Using Caldecotts Across the Curriculum

Reading and Writing Mini-lessons,
Math and Science Spin-offs,
Unique Art Activities,
and More!

by Joan Novelli

SCHOLASTIC
PROFESSIONAL BOOKS

NEW YORK • TORONTO • LONDON • AUCKLAND • SYDNEY

ACKNOWLEDGMENTS

All my thanks to Mary Beth Spann and Jeri Lynn Rea for lending their voices to the ideas in this book and to designer Jackie Swensen and illustrator James Hale for their creative talents. Special thanks to kindergarten, first, and second graders Dylan Novelli, Francesca Spann Minucci, James Spann Minucci, Elena Weinberg, Sara Weinberg, Jackson Berger, and the students in Donna Peabody's literacy group at Orchard School in South Burlington, Vermont, for brightening the pages of this book with their work.

Credits for illustrations and quotations that appear on the cover and interior pages of *Using Caldecotts Across the Curriculum*:

Make Way for Ducklings by Robert McCloskey. Copyright © 1941 by Robert McCloskey. Used by permission of Penguin USA.

The Little Island by Golden MacDonald, Leonard Weisgard, Illustrator. Copyright 1946 by Doubleday, a division of Bantam Doubleday Dell Publishing Group, Inc. Used by permission of Doubleday, a division of Bantam Doubleday Dell Publishing Group, Inc.

Finders Keepers by Will Lipkind, Nicolas Mordvinoff, Illustrator. Copyright © 1951 by Will Lipkind. Used by permission of Harcourt Brace & Co.

A Tree Is Nice Text Copyright © 1956 by Janice Udry. Text Copyright © renewed 1984 by Janice Udry. Pictures Copyright © 1956 by Marc Simont. Pictures Copyright © 1984 renewed by Marc Simont. Used by permission of HarperCollins Publishers.

Once a Mouse... by Marcia Brown. Copyright © 1961. Used by permission of Atheneum Books for Young Readers.

The Snowy Day by Ezra Jack Keats. Copyright © 1962. Used by permission of Penguin USA.

Arrow to the Sun by Gerald McDermott. Copyright © 1974 by Gerald McDermott. Used by permission of Penguin USA.

Why Mosquitoes Buzz in People's Ears retold by Verna Aardema, Leo and Diane Dillon, Illustrators. Copyright © 1975 by Verna Aardema. Used by permission of Penguin USA.

Ox-Cart Man by Donald Hall, Barbara Cooney, Illustrator. Copyright © 1979. Used by permission of Viking Children's Books.

Fables Copyright © 1980 by Arnold Lobel. Used by permission of HarperCollins Publishers.

The Glorious Flight by Alice and Martin Provensen. Copyright © 1983 by Alice and Martin Provensen. Used by permission of Penguin USA.

Saint George and the Dragon retold by Margaret Hodges, Trina Schart Hyman, Illustrator. Copyright © 1984 by Margaret Hodges. Used by permission of Little, Brown and Company.

Illustration by John Schoenherr reprinted by permission of Philomel Books from *Owl Moon* by Jane Yolen, illustrations copyright © 1987 by John Schoenherr.

From *Song and Dance Man* by Karen Ackerman, illustrated by Stephen Gammell. Text copyright © 1988 by Karen Ackerman. Illustrations copyright © 1988 by Stephen Gammell. Reprinted by permission of Alfred A. Knopf, Inc.

Cover illustration and lines by Ed Young. Reprinted by permission of Philomel Books from *Lon Po Po* by Ed Young. Copyright © 1988 by Ed Young.

Illustration by Emily Arnold McCully reprinted by permission of G. P. Putnam's Sons from *Mirette on the High Wire*, Copyright © 1992 by Emily Arnold McCully.

Grandfather's Journey by Allen Say. Copyright © 1993 by Allen Say. Used by permission of Houghton Mifflin Company.

Smoky Night by Eve Bunting, David Diaz, Illustrator. Copyright © 1994 by Eve Bunting. Used by permission of Harcourt Brace & Co.

Illustration by Peggy Rathman reprinted by permission of G. P. Putnam's Sons from *Officer Buckle and Gloria*, copyright © 1995 by Peggy Rathman.

Cover design by Jaime Lucero and Vincent Ceci
Interior design by Solutions by Design, Inc.
Interior illustrations by James Graham Hale

ISBN 0-590-11033-0

Contents

About This Book

A book is like a very small stage.

—MARCIA BROWN (*THE HORN BOOK*, JUNE 1967)

When I read aloud to my son, he sometimes interrupts with "Mama, can you please read with a little less expression?" (He wants to interpret the story himself.) Dylan immerses himself in the words and the pictures, soaking them in and using his imagination to bring stories to life. A story is like a stage for him—filled with fascinating people, interesting events, and magical places.

Caldecott winners, recognized as the most distinguished American picture books of their time, have a special power to bring stories to life. The art and the text in these books build on each other—together creating a complete story. Maurice Sendak's *Where the Wild Things Are* (HarperCollins, 1963) is a shining example. With spirited drawings, Sendak sweeps us away to a make-believe forest filled with wild things. And with his words "Let the wild rumpus start," we become wild things too. In *The Art of Maurice Sendak* (Abrams, 1980), Selma G. Lanes describes *Where the Wild Things Are* as "made not for the moment but for the ages." Like *Where the Wild Things Are*, other Caldecotts too are made "for the ages."

Go back to 1942 and *Make Way for Ducklings* (Viking, 1941), Robert McCloskey's beloved tale of a mallard family that decides to call Boston's Public Garden home. Expressive drawings invite us to follow along as the ducks waddle their way across crowded highways and down busy streets. More than half a century later, this story continues to delight children. The compelling story and commanding illustrations of *Smoky Night* (written by Eve Bunting, illustrated by David Diaz; Harcourt Brace, 1994) give this modern-day Caldecott the same timeless appeal. Like these favorites, Caldecotts make lasting impressions.

Classroom Connections

As a collection, Caldecotts are rich with teaching opportunities. From the striking Chinese panel art in *Lon Po Po: A Red Riding Hood Story From China* (by Ed Young; Philomel, 1989) to the stylized Pueblo Indian motifs in *Arrow to the Sun: A Pueblo Indian Tale* (by Gerald McDermott; Viking, 1974), Caldecotts introduce children to a wide range of illustration styles, inspiring their own artistic growth. The stories offer equally diverse possibilities for language arts lessons. *Fables* (written and illustrated by Arnold Lobel; HarperCollins, 1980) is full of delightful dialogue, modeling conventions of dialogue for students' own writing. *St. George and the Dragon* (written by Margaret Hodges, illustrated by Trina Schart Hyman; Little Brown, 1985) has page after page of wonderfully descriptive language—sure to inspire children's own word choice in writing. Other Caldecotts, old and new, abound with language-learning opportunities.

Caldecott classroom connections extend beyond art and language, enhancing learning across the curriculum. *Mirette on the High Wire* (written and illustrated by Emily Arnold; Putnam, 1992) offers lessons in tenacity and compassion. It's also a great book for introducing the science concepts of gravity and balance. *Grandfather's Journey* (written and illustrated by Allen Say; Houghton Mifflin, 1993) shares the crosscultural experiences of a family from Japan. And the winsome *Officer Buckle and Gloria* (written and illustrated by Peggy Rathman; Putnam, 1995) is just right for providing early safety instruction—raising awareness of other people's feelings at the same time.

These and other Caldecott stories are featured in the mini-units that make up this book. (The books appear in order from oldest to most recent, though you can use the units in any order you wish.) Here's a look at what's inside.

Book Quote: Like tiny poems, the quotes featured on the opening page of each mini-unit create images in your mind. You'll find activities that build on the quotes within the mini-units. More strategies for using these quotes as teaching tools follow.

One day a hermit sat thinking about big and little...
—FROM *ONCE A MOUSE...*

☀ Read the quote aloud to introduce the book. Ask children what they think the story will be about. Have them listen for the quote as you read the story.

☀ Copy and display the quotes (include titles and authors). Invite children to add to the display with favorite quotes from books they read. As children begin to notice how authors use language, they can use the samples as models for their own writing.

An Inside Look: Sharing information about authors and illustrators involves children on a more intimate level with books. From where ideas come from to how they're implemented, this section will give you insight into the work of illustrators and authors—information that will inspire teaching and learning

in your classroom. For example, Trina Schart Hyman, illustrator of *Saint George and the Dragon* (see page 74), says that she always begins a story by asking herself questions about characters and settings: "Who *are* these people? What do they like to eat for breakfast?…What time of year is it? What was the weather like?" (from her Caldecott acceptance speech) Learning to ask questions like these can help students develop an eye for the kind of detail that brings stories to life. Notes about other authors and illustrators suggest equally effective strategies.

An Art Lesson: Inspired by Caldecott books, these step-by-step projects invite children to explore the artist in themselves. Collage, easy printmaking, origami, maskmaking, and Chinese panel art are just a few of the art forms you'll find. (For more information about art in your classroom, see Close-Up on Art, page 7.)

[TIP] *Try the art projects yourself first so that you can get a feel for the process and make any changes necessary to meet your students' needs. You might also consider setting up these projects at stations to encourage independent exploration on their own.*

Language Arts Links: Suggestions for literature-inspired language experiences help you integrate reading, writing, speaking, and listening skills. (For more language arts links, see Language Arts Extras, pages 9–10.) Among other activities, this section includes:

☀ **Book Talk:** Encourage both personal responses and higher-level thinking with the discussion questions in this section.

☀ **Word Watch:** Like Jane Yolen's use of

figurative language in *Owl Moon* (Philomel, 1987), Caldecott books are full of inspiration for mini-lessons that bring students back to the story to introduce and reinforce language arts skills. Word clusters, compound words, synonyms, suffixes, prefixes, conventions of dialogue, onomatopoeia, alliteration, and descriptive language are just some of the areas covered.

❋ **Writer's Corner:** From a seasonal story wheel (see page 60) to a trunkful of jokes (see page 85), this section features fresh writing and publishing ideas.

Story Extensions: Engaging activities link stories and pictures to math, social studies, science, movement, and more. For example, you can introduce size comparisons with *Once a Mouse…* (by Marcia Brown; Scribner, 1961; see Big, Little, and More Ways to Measure, page 38), or set up a "high wire" in your classroom (yardsticks taped end to end on the floor) and explore the science concept of balance, which is brought to life in *Mirette on the High Wire.* (See A Balancing Act, page 95.)

Student Activity Pages: Reproduce these journal pages and templates to use with students.

Book Groups

One day, while visiting my son's kindergarten/first-grade class, I had the pleasure of observing an impromptu author/illustrator study. As the teacher prepared to share a story by Eric Carle, a child asked, "Is that the same person who wrote *A Snowy Day*?" "I think it's the person who wrote *The Very Hungry Caterpillar*," responded another. The discussion continued, with the children thoughtfully sharing comments about authors and their books for a mesmerizing few minutes.

Book groups (or author/illustrator studies) are a wonderful way to nurture children's love for literature and encourage them to make personal connections to books they read. Donna Peabody, a K–1 teacher at Orchard School in South Burlington, Vermont, suggests these strategies for organizing book groups with young children.

❋ Offer a choice of titles, if possible. For example, if you're reading *Officer Buckle and Gloria* (see page 109), set up groups to compare other titles by the same author.

❋ Model appropriate responses for book group discussions, encouraging respect for different ideas. Remind children to give one another "think time," too—time to let a child who is speaking formulate a thought without interruptions. (And when you notice children giving think time, be sure to compliment them.)

❋ Get children started by inviting them to look at the book cover. What connections can they make to other books by this author or illustrator?

❋ Have children keep response journals. Invite them to record reactions to a part of a story you want to draw their attention to. Other journaling ideas include free writing about favorite characters, recording words to describe characters or setting, and giving personal responses to an event in a story. Let children use their response journals to guide group discussions.

❋ Suggest that students use some of the same techniques you use in reading lessons to guide their discussions. They might make webs to organize details, use Venn diagrams to compare characters, or make lists of descriptive words, characters, and so on.

❋ Encourage parent involvement by asking them to help their children make lists of five all-time favorite books. Have children bring their lists to class and graph the data. Use the results to guide future child-generated author studies.

Close-Up on Art

Pablo Picasso once said, "I used to draw like Raphael, but it has taken me a whole lifetime to learn to draw like a child." (*From Awakening Your Child's Natural Genius* by Thomas Armstrong, Jeremy P. Tarcher, 1991). From early scribbles to drawings, paintings, and other forms of creative expression, children are naturally drawn to artistic experiences. As they see their artwork take shape, there's a growing feeling of accomplishment. Art experiences offer other benefits as well.

✷ Children can communicate and express themselves through art.

✷ As children try out their own creative ideas, they build self-confidence and grow as independent thinkers.

✷ Painting, drawing, sculpting, cutting, and other art skills strengthen eye-hand coordination—and pave the way for the fine motor skills that writing requires.

✷ Sharing artwork encourages appreciation of individual expression and differences.

You don't need to paint like Picasso to be able to guide children in their artistic endeavors. In fact, your own enthusiasm for art—whatever your perceived abilities—will go a long way in helping children develop positive attitudes about art. Keep in mind that children may not approach an art project the same way you might. The green grass in your collage might be blue in theirs. They may turn flowers into aliens from outer space. Allowing for individual interpretation will nurture their creative expression.

You can continue to encourage creativity in your responses to children's art. Rather than

And the Winner Is . . .

Of the thousands of new children's books published each year, only one wins the Caldecott Medal, awarded to the illustrator of the most distinguished picture book of the previous year. (The Caldecott is given in honor of nineteenth-century illustrator Randolph Caldecott.) If your children were on the committee to select the recipient of this award, which new book would they choose? Invite students to design and name their own award for favorite book of the year (for story, pictures, or both).

✷ To guide students in selecting a winner, create a simple form for rating new books. Ask students to record title, author, illustrator, and comments, and then rate the story and pictures on a scale of 1 to 5.

✷ When it's time to vote, let students work in small groups to narrow the field of favorites, with each group re-evaluating several titles and choosing a finalist.

✷ Bring students together for a final review, then vote! Plan a ceremony to celebrate your award winner and runners-up. Be sure to let the authors/illustrators know, too! To contact authors and illustrators, write their publishers' publicity departments.

praising the product ("What a lovely picture!"), focus on process and content: "I like the way you're experimenting with tones." or "The dog in your picture really looks like she's enjoying that bone." When you need to know more, you can always ask, "Can you tell me about...?" Most children will be happy to oblige! Finally, be sure to allow time for students to enjoy one another's artwork, for this is as important to the creative process as the artwork itself.

[TIP] *Let students work in teams of three to staff their art center—replacing supplies, cleaning up, and putting things where they belong.*

Resources

Books Kids Will Sit Still For by Judy Freeman (R. R. Bowker, 1996). The author, a school librarian, shares more than 2,000 favorite teacher- and child-tested titles plus 101 book-based activities.

Caldecott Medal Books, Volumes One and Two (*The Horn Book*). Caldecott acceptance speeches and illustrator biographies offer insight into the illustrators' lives and work. Check to see if your library lends these—you'll find many wonderful snippets to share.

The Horn Book. Full of reviews of children's books, articles by authors and illustrators, and more, this periodical also publishes Caldecott acceptance speeches. For information, call (800) 325-1170.

Meet the Authors and Illustrators: Volume One by Deborah Kovaks and James Preller (Scholastic Professional Books, 1991). Sixty authors and illustrators, including Caldecott winners Leo and Diane Dillon, Trina Schart Hyman, Robert McCloskey, Maurice Sendak, Ed Young, and Chris Van Allsburg talk about their work. Volume Two has sixty more,

including Caldecott winners Barbara Cooney, Paul Goble, Allen Say, and Peter Spier.

Newbery and Caldecott Medal Books, 1956–1965, 1966–1975, 1976–1985 (*The Horn Book*). See *Caldecott Medal Books.*

Read for the Fun of It: Active Programming With Books for Children by Caroline Feller Bauer (H. W. Wilson, 1992). Full of hints, how-to's, activities, games, and excerpts. The author's *This Way to Books* (H. W. Wilson, 1983) is also packed with ideas, suggestions, and techniques, including my favorite: "Remember your flood book." (Take a book with you wherever you go—you never know when you might have some time to pass.)

Writing With Pictures: How to Write and Illustrate Children's Books by Uri Shulevitz (Watson-Guptill Publications, 1985). Written by the illustrator of Caldecott Award-winner *The Fool of the World and the Flying Ship* (Farrar, Straus & Giroux, 1969).

OTHER

Kidstamps: Caldecott Award-winners David Diaz, Peggy Rathman, Maurice Sendak, Trina Schart Hyman, Leo and Diane Dillon, and Paul Goble are just a few of the favorite illustrators whose characters can be found on colorful rubber stamp sets available through Kidstamps, a company started by two librarians who wanted stamps of children's favorite book characters to use with their young readers. For a catalog, call (800) 727-5437.

Language Arts Extras

In addition to the language arts suggestions developed for each Caldecott book (see Language Arts Links, page 5) the following techniques can be used with any of the titles to enrich students' literature-based learning. Remember, too, that there will be times when you and your students just want to read a story for pure enjoyment. Try to find a balance so that students benefit from literature both as a source of simple pleasure and as a springboard for other learning.

CELEBRATING STORIES

Add to the excitement books generate by surprising children with your read-aloud selections. In *Read for the Fun of It: Active Programming With Books for Children* (H. W. Wilson, 1992), Caroline Feller Bauer suggests these attention-getters:

☀ Gift wrap the book you're reading. Children will await its unwrapping each day.

☀ Use a music stand to display the book. Drape a cloth over it. Unveil when you're ready to read.

☀ Dim the lights and shine a spotlight on the book as you introduce it.

STORY SACKS

Draw simple pictures that represent characters and events in a story. Place the pictures in a lunch bag and label it (title, author, and illustrator). Let children place pictures in sequential order to retell the story. Story sacks are fun for children to take home and share with families. (Try to build up a set of story stacks so that children can bring a new one home every couple of weeks.) Children will have fun making their own story sacks to share, too. (If drawing is not your thing, invite artistically inclined upper-grade students to help out. Let them sign their names to the bags.)

VOCABULARY STRETCHERS

Words like *chuckleberry* (from *The Little Island*, see page 17) and *cackling* (from *Fables*, see page 64) are just waiting to become part of your students' vocabularies. Here are some tips for inspiring your students to look for and learn new words.

☀ Let children act out their understanding of words—for example, *cackling* like the crow in *Fables*.

☀ After reading, invite children to suggest words for vocabulary mini-lessons. Often, these words will be just the ones you would have picked! Children can keep their own word lists, too, recording vocabulary from stories that they want to learn and use in their own writing.

SWBS CHARTS (SOMEBODY/WANTED/BUT/SO)

A technique that many teachers use to explore plot is the SWBS chart, which provides a structure for identifying key characters, what they want, what gets in their way, and how the problem is resolved. Adapt the sample shown here for books with a similar structure.

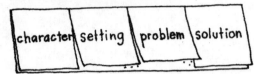

LIFT-THE-FLAP BOOKS

character	setting	problem	solution

Fold paper in half as shown and make three cuts in the top half to create four equal flaps. (12-by-18-inch paper gives children plenty of room to draw and write.) Use the four sections to examine a story. Suggestions follow.

❋ On the outside of each flap, ask students to describe a character using pictures and/or words. Underneath the flaps, have them write the names of the characters. Let children trade papers and try to guess the characters, lifting the flaps to check their answers.

❋ Organize flaps by story structure—for example, character, setting, problem, solution. Underneath each flap, have children draw pictures or use words to tell about each.

❋ Use the flaps for word-play activities. For example, to explore rhyme in *Make Way for Ducklings*, write words from the story (such as *quack, meet, swing, sleep*) on the outside of the flaps (one per flap). Underneath, ask children to write words that rhyme with each.

LISTS FOR LEARNING

Brainstorm lists based on stories you share—lists of unusual language (such as the alliteration in *Saint George and the Dragon*), rhyming words, characters' names, and so on. Use the lists as springboards for mini-lessons.

ACT IT OUT

Stories with a lot of dialogue, such as *Lon Po Po* (see page 87) and *Fables* (see page 64), make it easy to see who says what and therefore work well as mini-plays. Tips for helping students get the most out of acting experiences follow.

❋ Have students imagine that the play is like a movie. Can they picture each scene in their minds? Encourage use of expression and props to help the audience visualize the scene.

❋ To play more than one character, students can vary their voices and body language.

❋ Have students team up to practice projecting their voices. Can they hear one another from across a room?

❋ Share *Onstage & Backstage at the Night Owl Theater* by Anne Hayes (Harcourt Brace, 1997), a story that gives readers a behind-the-scenes look into theater as members of the Night Owl Theater prepare to perform *Cinderella*. Includes a stunning four-page fold-out spread and theater definitions.

❋ As a warm-up to acting out stories, invite children to use facial expressions to imitate characters in the story as you read. As they develop this mimetic skill, students will be able to show, often with great precision, how characters in stories feel.

Make Way for Ducklings

WRITTEN AND ILLUSTRATED BY
ROBERT MCCLOSKEY (VIKING, 1941)

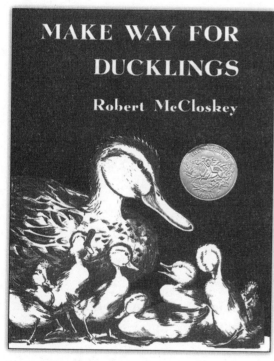

Mr. and Mrs. Mallard were looking for a place to live. But every time Mr. Mallard saw what looked like a nice place, Mrs. Mallard said it was no good.

—FROM *MAKE WAY FOR DUCKLINGS*

With foxes in the woods and turtles in the water, a duck can't raise a family just anywhere. So Mr. and Mrs. Mallard fly on and on until they come to the Charles River in Boston and declare it "just the right place." Hint: Have a duck call and police whistle handy for sound effects when you read this story aloud!

An Inside Look

Students who wonder "Could this really happen?" will be interested to hear the story behind Robert McCloskey's classic. "I first noticed the ducks when walking through the Public Garden every morning on the way to art school," he writes. "... I noticed the traffic problem of the ducks, and heard a few stories about them. Then the book just sort of developed from there." (from the book's back-flap copy)

To get the ducks in his drawings just right, McCloskey brought a few live mallards home. In *Meet the Authors and Illustrators: Volume One*, McCloskey says, "No effort is too great to find out as much as possible about the things you are drawing. It's a good feeling to be able to put down a line and know that it is right."

An Art Lesson

Like Robert McCloskey, children will discover that observing something up close can help them get the details just right in their own drawings. Though you may not be able to invite ducks into your classroom, students will be happy to bring in stuffed animals. (Or, if you have a class pet such as a fish or hamster, use that instead.)

Materials

* class pet or stuffed animals
* drawing paper
* colored pencils or pastels

[TIP] *To guide students in their drawings, introduce the concept of gesture drawings. Explain that a gesture drawing is like a quick scribble that shows the shape of what you're drawing. Let students make several gesture drawings of their animal(s) and then select one each to work into a drawing, darkening lines and adding details.*

If students are drawing stuffed animals, suggest that they turn them upside down. This will encourage them to draw what they see—instead of being distracted by what they think the animals are supposed to look like.

1 Have children observe their animal(s) from all sides. Ask questions to guide their observations. For example:

* How many legs (wings, paws, claws, and so on) does the animal have?
* Is this a soft, furry animal? Slimy? Prickly? Bumpy?
* What shades of light and dark do you see in this animal?
* How big is the animal? What object is about the same size?
* What shapes and patterns do you see?

2 Before students begin drawing, have them experiment with various drawing techniques. Look at the book for inspiration, noticing the following:

* the color of the illustrations (all done in shades of brown; children can use brown pencils to achieve a similar effect)
* shading (try smudging colored pencil or pastels with a finger or tissue)
* shadows (notice where real shadows fall)

3 Let children draw their animal(s), making several sketches until, like Robert McCloskey, they "know that it is right."

12

LANGUAGE ARTS LINKS

Book Talk

Make Way for Ducklings presents several problems and solutions as the ducks decide where to live and find their way around Boston's busy streets. After sharing the story, use these questions to help children recognize the problem-solution structure.

❋ What problem did Mr. and Mrs. Mallard have? (They couldn't agree on a place to live.)

❋ How did they solve it? (They kept looking until they found a place they both agreed was safe.)

❋ What problem did Mrs. Mallard have? (She had to get her baby ducks safely from the Charles River to the Public Garden.)

❋ How did she solve her problem? (She and her ducks kept quacking at the traffic until the police officer came and stopped traffic so that they could cross safely.)

❋ Ask children to share problems and solutions in their own lives. In the same way that Robert McCloskey wrote about a problem he saw (ducks in Boston's traffic), your students' own experiences with problems and solutions will make wonderful story starters.

Writer's Corner: Postcard Shop

Turn your writing center into a postcard shop. First, research places mentioned in the story, including the Public Garden, Beacon Hill, the State House, the Charles River, Louisburg Square, Charles Street, and Beacon Street. Find out about famous Bostonians, too, such as Ben Franklin, Paul Revere, and Louisa May Alcott. Then have children use the postcard pattern (see page 16) to draw and write about favorite places and people. Display postcards and invite other classes to "shop" at your stand.

Building on Books

Take a look at more of Robert McCloskey's stories and settings. Feel the sand in your toes and taste the salt in the air in *One Morning in Maine* (Viking, 1952; a Caldecott Honor book) and *Time of Wonder* (Viking, 1957; a Caldecott Medal book). Find Maine on a map and then locate places the author mentions, such as Penobscot Bay, Camden, Spectacle Island, Blastow's Cove, and Cape Rosier (all from *Time of Wonder*). Follow up by letting children tell about their own special places. This could be a park down the street or a favorite family vacation spot. Locate these places on maps too.

Word Watch: The *ack* Cluster

quack

Let ducklings Jack, Kack, Lack, Mack, Nack, Ouack, Pack, and Quack help children learn the letter cluster *ack* to help in decoding new words.

❊ Introduce the cluster by inviting children to make duck sounds. Write the word *quack* on the board. Ask: "What letters make the *ack* sound?" Underline the letters *ack*. Then reread the story, asking children to quack when they hear the ack sound. (They'll hear it in the ducklings' names and as the ducks step out onto a busy road: Qua-a-ack!! Quack! Quack! Quack! Quack!)

❊ Write *ack* words from the story on duck-shaped cards and use them to start a Ducks-in-a-Row display. Invite children to suggest other *ack* words, too.

❊ Leave duck patterns, blank paper, scissors, and pencils next to the display. Let children cut out duck-shaped cards to add more *ack* words on their own.

❊ What rhymes with *Jack*? Don't stop with his siblings' names. Follow up on Word Watch by letting children use the first letters of their names to make more names that rhyme with *Jack*. Have children write their new names on duck-shaped cards and display on their desks.

STORY EXTENSIONS

Math: Ducks in a Row

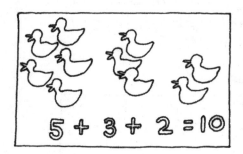

Ask students to count the number of ducks in the story (10). Ask: "If the ducks lined up in two equal rows, how many ducks would there be in each row?" Explore other configurations (7 and 3, 4 and 6, 2 and 8, and so on), including configurations for 3 rows. Have children draw and cut out ten ducks each (provide patterns to trace). Let them glue their ducks on blue construction paper in groups that combine to equal ten. Then have them write math sentences to represent their arrangements—for example $5 + 3 + 2 = 10$.

Social Studies: What Makes a Home?

Use the story as a springboard to learn more about homes. Begin by sharing the quote on page 11. Ask: "What did the ducks need in a home?" (water, food, safety from predators) "What do we need in our own homes?" Divide the class into groups, one for each kind of thing we need (such as food, clothing, and so on). Children can cut out pictures of these objects, paste them to poster paper, and label. When students are finished, discuss their choices. Encourage children to explain their reasoning and recognize the difference between things we need and things we want.

Science: A Symphony of Birds

Many children will tell you that ducks say *quack*. But what do other birds say? Share *Birdsong* by Audrey Wood (Harcourt Brace, 1997) to hear the sounds of birds among skyscrapers, in a garden, on a farm, in the woods, along a river, and more. For example, did you know that a kingfisher says *rickety-crick-crick, rickety-crick-crick*? A hummingbird says *chip-chee-chee*. A chickadee sounds like its name: *chick-a-dee-dee-dee*.

Follow up by writing the names and sounds of birds featured in the book on cards (duplicate if necessary so that you have one card per child). Punch two holes at the top of each and string with yarn so that children can wear cards around their necks. Let each child choose a card and practice the sound. (Students with the same sound can practice with one another.) Bring students together for a birdsong symphony!

Make Way for Ducklings

Cut out the postcard. Put paste on the back, then fold the postcard in half along the ------- line. On the front, draw a picture. In the upper left corner on the back, tell what your picture is. Add a message then address!

Front of postcard: Draw picture

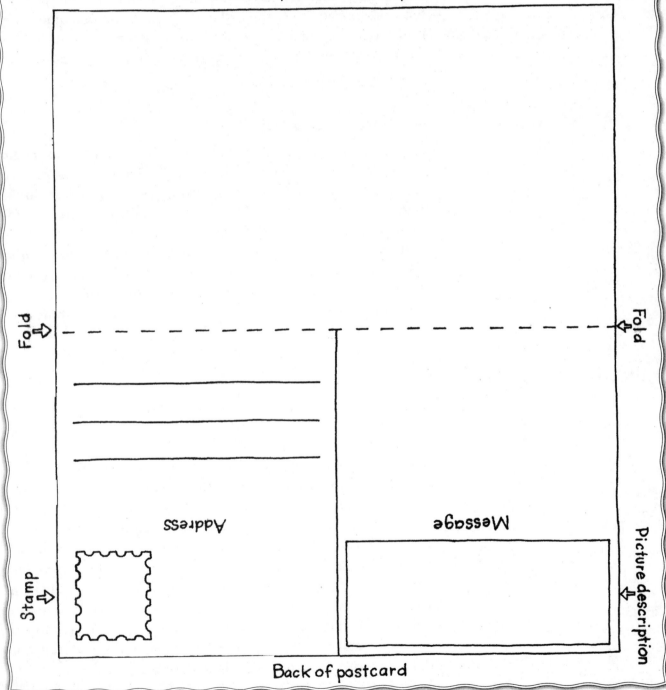

Back of postcard

The Little Island

WRITTEN BY GOLDEN MACDONALD
ILLUSTRATED BY LEONARD WEISGARD
(DOUBLEDAY, 1947)

This charming story shows seasonal changes that come to a little island in the ocean—from lobsters shedding their shells to snow falling softly in the night. Woven into the story is a gentle lesson about the interconnectedness of nature. (Margaret Wise Brown, who used the pen name Golden MacDonald for *The Little Island*, is the author of *Goodnight Moon* and more than 100 other books for children.)

The little Island had a little woods on it with seven big trees in it and seventeen small bushes and one big rock. Birds came to the woods on the Island and butterflies and moths flew over the ocean till they got there.

—FROM *THE LITTLE ISLAND*

An Inside Look

"We were all of us incredible creatures when we were little. We could see and hear and feel and smell and with easy concentration create things that never were and things that were yet to come…we could create a piece of silver out of some tinfoil…make a brown cow out of an old glove, build a city in the folds of a bed sheet, or even transform a doting aunt into a witch!" (from Weisgard's Caldecott acceptance speech) Leonard Weisgard captures this magical quality of childhood in his illustrations for *The Little Island*, where birds and butterflies visit, flowers bloom, seals raise their babies, birds build nests, strawberries turn red, storms come and go, and more.

Building on Books

For a closer look at the seasons, share *Fall*, *Winter*, *Spring*, and *Summer*, a series of nonfiction books by Ron Hirshi (Cobblehill). Each features full-color photographs that capture nature at its finest. Follow up by starting a class learning log to record students' observations of seasonal changes, including ways weather changes (and how students' clothing reflects this), how trees change, and how animals are affected. Invite students to take turns writing and drawing pictures in the log to record their observations. From time to time, revisit pages to help students understand the concept of seasonal change.

An Art Lesson

To illustrate *The Little Island*, Leonard Weisgard "took home" a little island off the coast of Maine—Vinalhaven. In his Caldecott acceptance speech, he says, "I saw this island grow tall or squat as the tides rose and fell. I've watched the mists blow in and hide the little island, sometimes leaving only the pine tree tops…I rowed to and from the little island with the seals swimming just below the surface of the water; I've seen the sun rise and make a golden island for just five seconds in an early morning sea….I took it home to Connecticut, and remembered it in my own way."

What place in nature would each of your students enjoy "taking home" to illustrate? This book-making activity guides children in illustrating memories of favorite places—a beach, a backyard, or whatever comes to mind. (As a warm-up to this activity, try Book Talk, page 19.)

Materials

* white paper (5 sheets per child)
* stapler
* scissors
* crayons, markers

1 Ask questions designed to help children picture their places. For example:

* What do you see when you think of this place?

* Are there plants growing here? Animals?

* What are some ways this place changes in summer, fall, winter, and spring?

* Can you imagine the sun coming up here? What would you see?

2 Help children make books to illustrate their special places in each season. For each book, staple together five sheets of white paper across the top. Cut one inch from the bottom of page four, two inches from page three, three inches from page two, and four inches from the top page so that the pages are staggered, as shown.

My Backyard
by James
winter
spring
summer
fall

3 Have each child illustrate a cover on the top page and then write the name of each season on the bottom of the remaining four pages.

4 Let children illustrate their picture books, depicting their places in each season.

Leonard Weisgard's illustrations for *The Little Island* were rendered in gouache (opaque watercolor). To make an inexpensive substitute, try mixing a few teaspoons of white glue with about a cup of tempera paint. The paint will dry with a glossy finish and will also resist cracking.

LANGUAGE ARTS LINKS

Book Talk

Guide children in recognizing the cycle of seasons portrayed in this book by taking a closer look at the pictures. As you turn the pages, ask:

* What season do you think this is? What are some clues?

* How are the seasons here like the seasons where we live? How are they different?

* If you were going to add on to the story of this little island, what season would your part of the story take place in? Why?

Writer's Corner: Island Life

Make a mural that invites children to become experts on the little island and the world around it.

* Begin by making a list of all the plants and animals on and around the island, such as lobster, bats, butterflies, seals, violets, wild strawberries, and kingfishers.

* Let students team up and choose one of the plants or animals to research. Guide their research by asking "What do you already know about your plant/animal? What would you like to find out?" Have students create pictures and reports about their plants and animals.

* Together, paint an island scene on craft paper. Let students add their pictures and reports to the mural.

Word Watch: Descriptive Language

howling   moaning   whistling

The Little Island is full of vivid words, such as those that describe the wind in a storm. Locate sentences in the story that feature especially descriptive words and write them on sentence strips, leaving blanks where the adjectives go. Let children suggest words to complete each of the sentences. Write each word on a card. Place sentence strips and cards in a pocket chart. Then let children take turns placing different words in the blanks and reading the sentences aloud. Discuss how the meaning changes with each new word. Follow up by filling in the author's word choic-

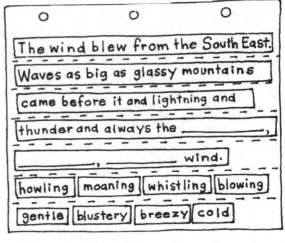

es. How do these words change the feel of the sentence? Continue to build awareness of language by asking children to look for and point out descriptive words in their own writing.

STORY EXTENSIONS

Science: My Little Island

What is an island? Let students share their ideas and then build islands of their own to learn how "all land is one land under the sea." (from *The Little Island*)

1 After sharing the story, ask children to tell what they know about islands. Guide them to understand that an island is surrounded entirely by water but that the land they see is not floating on water—it is part of a land formation that reaches to the bottom of the body of water.

2 Give each child a set of materials (bowl, handful of plasticine, assorted island objects) and let them make islands in their bowls. Make sure that their islands have some height to allow for water in the bowl.

Materials

❋ clear plastic bowls

❋ plasticine

❋ twigs, pine needles, small stones, and other objects from nature

❋ water

❋ plastic animals

❋ toy boats (for origami boats, see page 101)

20

3 Have children pour water into their bowls so that the tops of their islands remain above water. Then let them add toy boats to complete their island scenes.

4 Invite children to look at their islands from the top and sides to see the land formation above and below the water line. Ask them what they think the author meant when she said, "All land is one land under the sea."

Math: An Island of Numbers

Use *The Little Island* to give children experiences in number concepts. Using the quote on page 17, let children pretend to be the trees and bushes to discover how many there are altogether on the island. Or let them use twigs to represent the correct number of trees and bushes on their island models. (See My Little Island, page 20.) Follow up by having students write their own math problems based on the story. (For example, How many different kinds of flying animals are there? How many different kinds of animals altogether make their home on or around the island?) Let children share their problems. Again, have them act out problems and solutions or show their work and explain their reasoning.

Movement/Language Arts: Windy Ways

Wind is a part of life on the little island. Select some appropriate music to play while you describe different types of windy conditions for children to act out. (Vivaldi's *The Four Seasons* is a good choice.) For example, can students move like a gentle wind—one that blows spiderwebs without breaking them? How about a howling wind? Start a class dictionary of wind and other weather words, making tabs to organize entries by categories (wind, clouds, rain, and so on). The next time students need weather words for a story, remind them to look here!

Finders Keepers

WRITTEN BY WILL LIPKIND
ILLUSTRATED BY NICOLAS MORDVINOFF
(HARCOURT BRACE, 1951)

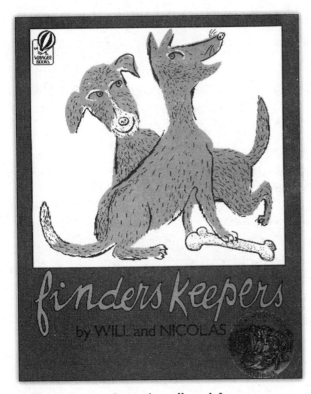

*"That bone is mine," said
Nap. "I saw it first."
"It's mine," said Winkle.
"I touched it first."*
—FROM FINDERS KEEPERS

Two dogs find a bone—one seeing it first, the other touching it first—and can't agree on who it belongs to. They ask a farmer and a goat and a barber to help them decide who should have it. At last they meet a big dog, whose own ideas about the bone quickly prompt Nap and Winkle to agree that sharing one bone is better than having none at all.

An Inside Look

Nicolas Mordvinoff collaborated with his friend Will Lipkind on *Finders Keepers*. In his Caldecott acceptance speech, Mordvinoff said that though one draws and the other writes, "we work in such a close relationship that when a book is finished, it is sometimes hard for us to remember who was responsible for what idea." Students may notice that some pages are illustrated in three colors, others in two colors. As with *A Tree Is Nice* (see page 27) and other books of this time, this was sometimes a factor of printing costs. (Printing pages in two colors is less expensive.)

An Art Lesson

Materials

* scrap paper
* colored pencils, crayons
* drawing paper

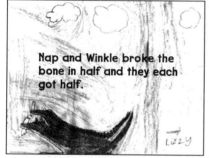

This story ends with Will and Nap fighting the big dog for the bone. Invite students to write and illustrate a different kind of ending, one that implements some of the conflict resolution strategies they've learned. Let them team up like Nicolas and Will to put story and pictures together.

1 Have each team begin by discussing and sketching ideas. Guide this part of the process by asking the following questions:

* How will the dogs resolve their problem?

* How will the pictures show this?

* What colors will you use?

* Where will the words go on the page? The picture? (Explain that this is part of designing a page.)

2 Have children make "dummies" of their pages, starting with miniatures and then going to full-size paper when they're satisfied with the story, pictures, color, and so on.

3 Display students' alternative endings along with the book. Celebrate children's teamwork by inviting them to share how they worked together to create their new endings. Encourage them to talk about any problems they encountered and how they resolved them.

LANGUAGE ARTS LINKS

Book Talk

Invite children to discuss *Finders Keepers* by asking questions that encourage higher-level thinking and personal response. Let children contribute their own discussion questions, too.

* What problem does the author use to start the story and make you want to keep reading?

* Has this kind of problem ever happened to you? What would you do if you and a friend found something and you both wanted to keep it?

* Did the story end the way you thought it would? What might have happened if the big dog hadn't come along?

Word Watch: -ed Endings

touched   **pushed**   **pulled**

Finders Keepers is full of *-ed* endings, beginning with *touched* ("I touched it first."). Plan a mini-lesson to teach this ending, writing a couple of sentences from the book on the board and asking: "What do you notice about these sentences?"

Invite volunteers to come up to the board to draw lines between root words and *-ed* endings. Follow up by making flip-flap word strips for children.

❊ Write words that end in *-ed* on strips of paper (one word per strip).

❊ Draw a dotted line between the root word and the ending.

❊ Fold the strips back on the dotted line. Let children read the words both ways, unfolding the flaps to add the *-ed* ending.

❊ Provide blank strips for children to make their own flip-flap word strips to share.

Plan a similar mini-lesson to introduce the suffix *-ing. Digging, waggling, clipping,* and *snipping* are just some of the words from the story you can use.

Story Circle

Finders Keepers has a very clear sequence—the dogs find a bone and then ask, in order, a farmer, a goat, a barber, and a big dog for help in deciding who the bone belongs to. Let students prepare to retell the story by making story circles following these steps:

❊ Use a paper plate to trace a circle on paper. Cut it out.

❊ Draw pictures around the circle to show the events in order from beginning to end. (See the illustration below.)

[TIP] *Keep in mind that some students may have more parts to their circles than others, depending on how many details they provide. Invite students to use their story circles as guides to retell the story aloud.*

Writer's Corner: Who Said What

"That's mine!" "No, it's mine!" *Finders Keepers* is sure to inspire lively discussions about times students have argued about possessions—making this a compelling writing topic. It's also a perfect opportunity to introduce the use of quotation marks. Begin by copying a few lines from the story, minus the quotation marks. (Use the quote on page 22 for starters.) Model where to put quotation marks, then let children take turns filling in more. Next, write down a brief classroom conversation, again leaving out the quotation marks and letting students fill them in. Then have children tell their own Finders Keepers stories based on discussions they've had with friends or siblings about possessions—using quotation marks to show who said what.

STORY EXTENSIONS

Social Studies: Cooperating and Compromising

Use the quote on page 22 to get students thinking about times they too have argued over possessions. Explore the concepts of cooperation and compromise by role-playing some of these situations. First, write situations that come up at home or at school on cards. (If you've done the Writer's Corner activity, above, you can use students' stories for ideas.) Then let children work in teams to role-play them. Note: This is a good time to discuss how Nap and Winkle fight to get their bone back in the end. Ask: "If Nap and Winkle were really two children and the bone was a toy, what are some other ways they could solve their problem?"

Math: How Many Pets?

After reading *Finders Keepers*, students will be eager to share their own pet stories. Help students design a survey to find out more about pets. Start with one everyone can participate in: Do you have a pet? Let children make a bar graph to show results, writing their names above Yes or No to indicate their responses. Follow up with other surveys and graphs to learn more, for example, "Pets We Wish We Could Have" or "Number of Pets in Our Home," both of which will allow all students (regardless of whether or not they actually have pets) to participate. Discuss

Do you have a pet?	
Masami	Raj
Sasha	Ruby
Sara	Sawyer
Dylan	
Meghan	
Jackson	
Yes	No

completed graphs. Guide students in interpreting the data by asking questions such as:

* Which column has the most names in it? What does this mean?

* Which column has the fewest names in it? What does this mean?

* Are there more dogs or cats?

* Are there fewer birds or snakes?

* How many fewer/more pet fish are there than pet cats?

* How many pets are there altogether?

Ask: "How does organizing information, or data, on a graph make it easier to understand?"

Building on Books

Finders Keepers is a trickster tale of sorts, though the trickster in this story doesn't succeed. "This is a nice little bone," the big dog tells Nap and Winkle, as he offers to take care of it for them. He almost gets away with the trick, but Nap and Winkle wise up and get the bone back. Explore other trickster tales, such as Julius Lester's retellings of the Uncle Remus stories.

* *The Tales of Uncle Remus: The Adventures of Brer Rabbit* (Dial, 1987)

* *More Tales of Uncle Remus: Further Adventures of Brer Rabbit, His Friends, Enemies, and Others* (Dial, 1988)

* *Further Adventures of Uncle Remus: The Misadventures of Brer Rabbit, Brer Fox, Brer Wolf, the Doodang, and Other Creatures* (Dial, 1990)

* *The Last Tales of Uncle Remus* (Dial, 1994)

A Tree Is Nice

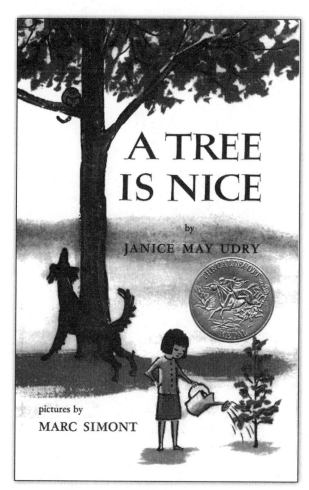

A tree is nice because it has a trunk and limbs. We can climb the tree and see over all the yards. We can sit on a limb and think about things. Or play pirate ship up in the tree.

—FROM *A TREE IS NICE*

WRITTEN BY JANICE MAY UDRY
ILLUSTRATED BY MARC SIMONT
(HARPERCOLLINS, 1956)

From trees that fill the sky to one tiny tree newly planted, here is a book full of reasons for appreciating trees.

An Inside Look

As you share this book with children, notice together that the illustrations alternate between four colors and black and white. Compare with other books from around the same time, such as *The Little Island*. (See page 17.) Ask children to speculate about why some of the pages in these books are illustrated in two colors. One simple explanation is that printing pages in color costs more than black and white.

In his Caldecott acceptance speech, Marc Simont compares his approach to illustrating to what children do every day in their art. "Although we are forever amazed at the beautiful pictures children can make, still, their intention is not to make a beautiful picture at all, but to tell a story. You've seen them, huddled over a piece of paper with crayon in hand, muttering fantastic doings to themselves—'and the lion comes running down the hill, and the cowboy is galloping on his horse…'" Simont's illustrations for *A Tree Is Nice* complement the childlike charm of the story beautifully.

Building on Books

Take a close-up look at one special tree with *Sky Tree* by Thomas Locker (HarperCollins, 1995). Like Udry, Locker has a special feeling for trees. In an author's note he says, "I have spent most of my life learning to paint trees against the ever changing sky. After all these years I still cannot look at a tree without being filled with a sense of wonder."

Sky Tree expresses that wonder through illustrations and text that show how one tree can be so many things—a snug home for squirrels, a resting place for birds in winter, a nesting place when they return in spring. Let students adopt a tree to observe over time. As a class students can record observations of the tree at different times of the day, under different weather conditions, and as seasons come and go. Each season, invite children to illustrate scenes that show how the tree changes. Put the pages together to make a book about their tree.

An Art Lesson

In *A Tree Is Nice*, Janice May Udry paints pictures of many different kinds of trees—trees for climbing, trees for shade, trees for apples, for hanging swings on, for picnicking under, for protecting houses from winds. Let children illustrate stories about trees they are familiar with and then share their stories.

Materials

* crayons, colored pencils
* paint, paintbrushes
* paper

1 Spark students' ideas with these questions.

* What kinds of trees grow where you live?

* Have you ever seen a tree with a trunk too big to put your arms around?

* What birds have you seen in trees? What other animals have you seen in trees?

* Does anyone have a favorite tree for climbing? For playing hide-and-seek?

* Has anyone ever planted a baby tree?

2 Once everyone has a tree story to illustrate, let students choose a medium (crayon, paint, pencil, and so on) and begin. Share these suggestions to inspire students' imaginations. Invite children to add their own ideas, too.

* Take a look at a real tree to see how branches grow (up and out toward the light). Notice the shape of the tree (its trunk, leaves, branches) and its colors.

* Suggest that students consider the following questions: What season is it in your picture/story? What colors are

I like my tree because it is my favorite tree. It has a rainbow over it. Sophie

the leaves of your tree in this season? Are there pale green buds? Red-orange leaves ready to fall? Deep green needles on an evergreen? What's happening around your tree?

☀ Ask students to describe the sky they see out the window. Ask: "How could you paint a sky like this in your picture?" Discuss techniques for creating other kinds of skies—for example, blending the edges with your finger to make soft clouds, dabbing tiny bits of white paint on leaves to indicate sunlight, brushing light gray paint unevenly over the paper to show a misty day.

3 Invite students to write stories to go with their pictures.

LANGUAGE ARTS LINKS

Book Talk

After sharing the story, let students recall all the reasons Janice May Udry gives for trees being nice. Let students add reasons of their own. Write these on the board or on a construction-paper tree. Questions to guide further discussion follow.

☀ What are some things we use that come from trees?

☀ What kinds of trees give us food to eat?

☀ Do you know how trees help make the air we breathe?

☀ How do other things in nature help us? (For example, rain helps plants grow, makes puddles to play in, and helps keep rivers and lakes from drying up.)

Writer's Corner: Collaborative Tree Guide

[TIP] *Have children write information about their trees on scrap paper first. Then edit and revise to make captions for their photo pages.*

Make a collaborative tree guide by letting children photograph different trees and research to find out about them (name, leaf type, average height, and so on). You can photograph trees around school or send a disposable camera home with students to take photos of trees in their neighborhoods. (Parents can photograph their children with the trees.) Have children use glue or photo corners to affix their photos to heavy paper. Then let them add information about their trees and bind pages with O-rings.

Word Watch: Descriptive Language

nice

The word *nice* often appears in lists of words children are told not to use in their writing. It's a word that usually doesn't do much to paint a vivid picture. But in *A Tree Is Nice*, the word becomes part of the story's poetic appeal. Rather than rule out some words in children's writing, help them discover alternatives so that they can choose language that best describes what they want it to. Here, children grow new words for *nice* on mini-trees.

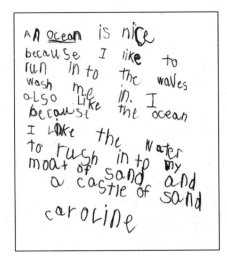

1. Let children take turns painting their arms from the inside of their elbows to their palms and fingertips and print them on craft paper. These prints will be their trees.

2. Write "A tree is _____ ." on the board. Have children write synonyms for *nice* on construction-paper leaves (they can tear or cut paper to make them) and glue them to their trees.

3. As children come across more synonyms for *nice*, let them add new leaves (and branches if they want) and watch their trees grow!

Nature Lovers

The simplicity of *A Tree Is Nice* will appeal to children, who can use the story as a model for their own stories about nature (for example, the sun, rain, rivers, and so on). Help children get started by using the repetitive language of *A Tree Is Nice* as a model.

_____ are very nice. They _____.

Have children tell why the things they are writing about are nice.

A̲n̲ o̲c̲e̲a̲n̲ is nice because I like to run in to the waves also like in. I because the ocean I LIKe the water to rush in to my moat of sand a castle of sand

caroline

STORY EXTENSIONS

Math/Science: Specimen Sort

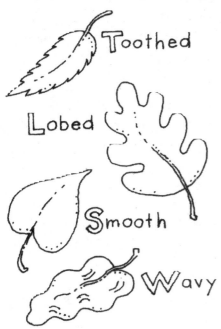

Toothed

Lobed

Smooth

Wavy

Scientists classify leaves by characteristics such as leaf edge (toothed, smooth, wavy, lobed). As a warmup to a leaf classification activity, try this game. Without telling children your sorting rule, divide them into two groups—for example wearing sneakers/not wearing sneakers. Say: "Pretend I'm a scientist and I am studying you. I've just sorted you into two groups. Can you guess what is the same about the children in each group?" (Be aware that children may notice a different characteristic than the one you had in mind.) Let children offer their ideas and then take turns sorting classmates according to their own rules.

Follow up by going on a leaf-collecting walk, picking up specimens from the ground. (Gather some yourself, making sure you collect some that represent a variety of leaf edges.) Back in the classroom, let your scientists work in small groups to sort leaves. Take time to let each group try to guess the others' sorting rules. Finally, if students haven't already sorted by edges, help them do so. Use the leaves again in the art activity that follows.

Art: Leaf-Printed Paper

[TIP] *To help children keep their work area neat, cover work surfaces with newspaper. Children can just lift off sheets of newspaper when they need a clean surface.*

Many children will be familiar with the process of making leaf rubbings: placing paper over a leaf and rubbing crayon over the surface to pick up the shape of the leaf, its vein structure, and so on. Introduce another way to print with leaves: painting the surface of the leaf (vein side up), placing paper on top, rubbing with the edge of your hand, then lifting off the paper to reveal the print. A framed series of leaf prints makes a wonderful gift!

Science/Math: Leaves Line Up

Materials
* leafy twigs
* journal page (see page 33)
* sugar cookie dough
* leaf-shaped cookie cutters
* food coloring, sprinkles

What patterns form as leaves grow on stems? Gather some leafy twigs and let children find out! Look for leafy twigs after a windy or rainy day. Make sure the twigs are long enough for students to observe a repeating pattern.

1 Gather children in a circle and pass around one of the twigs. Ask children to notice the way the leaves are growing.

2 Draw a picture of the twig on the board, filling in just the first few leaves. Invite children to take turns adding leaves

to continue the pattern. Encourage them to describe the pattern the leaves form.

3 Share the names scientists use to describe leaf patterns. In addition to *simple* leaf patterns (leaves attached directly to the stalk), you may see examples of *compound* leaf patterns (leaflets on petioles attached to a twig in a pattern.) Use the journal page to reinforce students' understanding.

4 Make leafy treats to eat! Divide the class into groups. Have each group form a twig with cookie dough. Give each child a chunk of dough to make a leaf-shaped cookie, using food coloring or sprinkles to add color. Add leaves to the twigs to form patterns. Bake and enjoy!

[TIP] *For a fun, interactive science center activity, display leafy twigs and pattern blocks. Model the activity by using the blocks to represent one of the leaf patterns. Can students match your pattern with the twig? Let children use the blocks themselves to represent leaf patterns. Can they match one another's patterns with the twigs?*

Science: Adopt a Tree

Learn more about trees by adopting one in your school's backyard. Take seasonal walks to the tree to observe changes. Keep a class journal to record observations in pictures and words. Questions to investigate include:

‑ Is the tree evergreen or deciduous?

‑ About how tall is the tree?

‑ How old do you think the tree is? What are some clues?

‑ What are its leaves like (type and pattern)?

‑ What are some words to describe the tree?

‑ What do you notice around your tree? How does this change with the seasons?

JOURNAL PAGE

Leaves Line Up

Find the leaf pattern on each twig. Draw more leaves like this on each twig.

Look at a twig of your own. Use the back of this paper to draw the leaf pattern.

Once a Mouse...

WRITTEN AND ILLUSTRATED BY **MARCIA BROWN**
(SCRIBNER, 1961)

*One day a hermit
sat thinking about
big and little—*
  —FROM *ONCE A MOUSE...*

Follow the magical adventures of a mouse in a faraway forest and, like the hermit in this retelling of a fable from India, ponder the meaning of *big* and *little*.

An Inside Look

With three colors—yellow, green, and red—Marcia Brown, a three-time Caldecott winner, created the simple but striking woodcut illustrations in *Once a Mouse....* In *The Illustrator's Notebook*, edited by Lee Kingman (The Horn Book, 1978), she explains her choices. "The story of *Once a Mouse...* moves in an arc from quietness to quietness; from meditation, to concern, to involvement, to anger and action, back to meditation. The colors I chose were the yellow-green of sun through leaves, of earth, the dark green of shadows, and the red that says India to me. Red is used as a force to cut into the other colors when its violence is needed."

An Art Lesson

Materials

* foam trays, corrugated cardboard
* pencils
* paintbrushes, craft sticks, toothpicks, and other tools for carving
* tempera paint
* small rollers or paintbrushes
* paper

[TIP] *For more simple printmaking, try this technique: Lightly coat a tray or other surface with paint. Place a sheet of paper on top of the paint, then use a pencil to draw a design. Lift the paper to reveal the print.*

Building on Books

Set up a printmaking studio in your classroom! First, gather together some children's books illustrated in woodcut. In addition to *Once a Mouse…*, fine examples include:

* *Tracks in the Wild* written and illustrated by Betsy Bowen (Little, Brown, 1993)
* *A Story A Story*, illustrated by Gail E. Haley (Atheneum, 1970; Caldecott winner)

Invite students to notice where the illustrators cut away wood for each picture. Then guide students in following these steps to make prints of their own.

1 Lightly sketch a design on a foam tray or a piece of corrugated cardboard.

2 For a foam tray, use the tip of a paintbrush, a craft stick, or another tool to scratch away the areas outside the design, leaving a raised positive image (the part that prints). If you're printing with cardboard, peel away the cardboard around the design.

3 Use a brush or roller to cover the block with paint, being careful not to get paint in the areas that have been carved away.

4 Place the painted side of the block on paper, press gently, then lift off to reveal the image.

In addition to winning Caldecotts for *Once a Mouse…*, *Shadow* (Scribner, 1982), and *Cinderella* (Scribner, 1954), Marcia Brown also illustrated six Caldecott Honor books, including *The Steadfast Tin Soldier* (Scribner, 1953), *Puss In Boots* (Scribner, 1952), *Skipper John's Cook* (Scribner, 1951), *Dick Whittington and His Cat* (Scribner, 1950), *Henry Fisherman* (Atheneum, 1949), and *Stone Soup* (Scribner, 1947). Create a display featuring her work. Let students compare the stories and art in these books using charts or graphic organizers.

LANGUAGE ARTS LINKS

Book Talk

Once a Mouse... has a surprising ending: after turning the mouse into progressively bigger animals so he could protect himself, the hermit turns him back into a mouse when he senses that the mouse is ungrateful. Use the ending to initiate a discussion. Sample discussion starters follow.

 ❋ Did the ending surprise you? What would you have done with the mouse if you were the hermit?

 ❋ Pretend you're the mouse. Say something to convince the tiger to give you a second chance.

 ❋ What do you think the moral of the story is?

 ❋ Make up a new ending. This time have the mouse behave in a way that would make the hermit feel good about his decision to turn the mouse into a tiger.

Writer's Corner: Words Paint Pictures

In *Once a Mouse...*, the animals don't just move, they *leap*, *prowl*, and *peacock*! This story is full of other descriptive words—*snatched*, *mighty*, *stout*, and *wretched*—making it a perfect springboard for a mini-lesson on word choices.

 ❋ Start by writing a sentence from the story on the board, leaving a blank in place of a descriptive verb.

 > "Not long after that, a hungry tiger was
 > _____ in the forest, and leaped on the dog."

 ❋ Invite students to suggest verbs to fill in the blank. Read the sentence each time, using their words to fill in the blank. How do the meaning and mood change with each word choice?

 ❋ Fill in the word from the story (*prowling*). Ask: "What kind of picture does this word paint?"

 ❋ Encourage children to use *Once a Mouse...* as a model for their own writing. In conferencing with students, ask: "Which words in your story help paint pictures? Which ones could be stronger?"

Word Watch:
Adding un-

ungrateful

Use words from the story to introduce a mini-lesson on the prefix *un-*. For example, write the word *ungrateful* on the board. Let a student underline the root word. Ask: "When we add the letters *un* to the word *grateful*, how does the meaning change?" Let students suggest other words beginning with *un*. Using the illustration as a guide, make word pull-throughs so that students can build and read their words.

Circular Stories

Once a Mouse... has a circular story structure—the hermit begins and ends by "thinking about big and little." Help children recognize this structure by writing the basic parts of the story on sentence strips. Draw simple pictures to go along with the words. Give each child one of the sentence strips. Then invite children to work together to arrange themselves in a circle to retell the story from beginning to end. Reread the story to check the order.

A Game of Opposites

The hermit in *Once a Mouse...* is thinking about *big* and *little*. Share the quote from the story on page 34 to introduce these opposites. Brainstorm other opposites such as *dark* and *light*, *near* and *far*, *hot* and *cold*, *right* and *left*, *front* and *back*, and *fast* and *slow*. Record students' suggestions on a chart and display. You might also copy the opposites on index cards and place them in a basket. Let small groups of students use the cards to play a matching game, mixing up the cards and placing them facedown on the floor or a table. Have students take turns turning over two cards to try to match opposites. For easy self-checking, students can refer to the chart.

STORY EXTENSIONS

Science/Movement: Animals on the Move

In *Once a Mouse...*, the tiger *peacocks* about the forest. Look at pictures of peacocks (noticing how the tail feathers fan out) and talk about the expression "proud as a peacock." Ask: "What do you think a tiger that peacocks about would look like?" Then invite students to peacock about the room. Follow up by investigating other animal movements. For example, what does a snake slithering look like? A cat prowling? A chipmunk scurrying? An elephant lumbering? Let students take turns prowling, peacocking, and otherwise moving about like various animals. Who can guess what they are?

Science: Predator or Prey?

Once a Mouse... introduces children to the life of a forest, where a watchful eagle eyes a tiny mouse and a hungry tiger preys on a dog. Explore predator-prey relationships by having students retell the story, substituting animals that live near them. What tiny animal can students substitute for the mouse? For the eagle, cat, dog, and tiger? Assist students in conducting simple research to learn more about the animals before having them decide the sequence of their stories. (For example, a worm could be turned into a big bird, which could change into a cat, which could change into a dog.) Invite students to illustrate and share their stories.

Math: Big, Little, and More Ways to Measure

Using the categories *big* and *little* is one way to compare size. What other ways can students find? Introduce this activity by listing animals in the story from big to little. Then brainstorm a list of other animals. Let each student choose one to research, using the journal page to record information. (See page 39.) Have students take turns sharing their discoveries. Then work together to make more size comparisons. Suggestions follow.

- ※ Group animals by shorter/longer than a pinkie finger (or other nonstandard unit of measurement).

- ※ Group by weight: less than/more than/about the same as a child in the class.

- ※ Group by thinner/wider than some unit of measurement.

Social Studies: Story Map

The story of *Once a Mouse...* originated in India. Display a world map (the simpler the better) and have children locate India. Ask a child to draw a picture that represents *Once a Mouse...* and use a pushpin to attach it to the map. Each time you share a folktale, place a new picture on the map to mark its place of origin. How many places will you visit this year without leaving your classroom?

JOURNAL PAGE

Big, Little, and More Ways to Measure

1. The animal I am learning about is _____.

2. This animal is (big, little) _____.

   This is why I think so. _____

   _____

   _____

   _____

3. My animal is (longer, shorter) than my pinky finger.

   _____

4. I can describe the size of my animal another way.

   _____

   _____

   _____

5. I can find three things that are the same size as my animal.

   _____

   _____

   _____

The Snowy Day

WRITTEN AND ILLUSTRATED BY EZRA JACK KEATS
(VIKING, 1962)

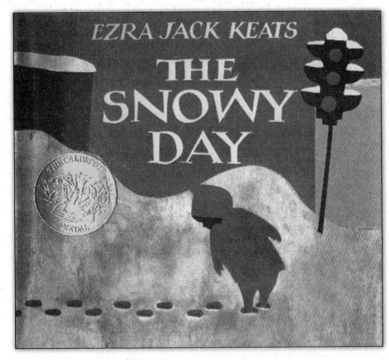

Peter awakens to a world of snow. He makes tracks and snow angels, goes sliding, and packs snowballs—saving one in his pocket for the next day. Keats' simple story and collage illustrations capture a child's natural wonder for the world in a book that charms readers of all ages.

An Inside Look

The young child in this story was inspired by photographs of a boy in *Life* magazine that Ezra Jack Keats clipped and hung on his studio wall. "His expressive face, his body attitudes, the very way he wore his clothes, totally captivated me," he said in his Caldecott acceptance speech. In a biographical note by Esther Hautzig (*Newbery and Caldecott Medal Books: 1956–1965*), Keats recalls his beginnings as an artist. He was nine or ten and had filled up the surface of the kitchen table with drawings. "My mother came in and I expected her to say, '… Get that sponge and wash it off!' Instead she looked at me and said, 'Did you do that? Isn't it wonderful!'"

Crunch, crunch, crunch, his feet sank into the snow. He walked with his toes pointing out...
He walked with his toes pointing in...
—FROM THE SNOWY DAY

40

Meet up with Peter again as you share *Whistle for Willie* (Viking, 1964), also illustrated in collage. Peter, who longs to be able to whistle for his dog, "blew till his cheeks were tired." Suddenly, when he's least expecting it, out comes the whistle. Follow up by letting children whistle for pretend pets in the classroom. They'll enjoy telling their own tales about how they learned to whistle, too. For a fun follow-up, let children write or dictate stories about how they accomplished some other goal—like blowing bubbles with gum or tying shoes.

An Art Lesson

Collage is an art form that appeals to young children. From soft cotton balls to slippery candy wrappers, collage materials have a limitless range of textures—inviting the tactile experiences many children thrive on. Take a close-up look at the colorful pages in *The Snowy Day*. Can children guess how the illustrator made the gray background on pages where Peter is sleeping? (ink spattered with a toothbrush) The snowflakes? (patterns cut from gum erasers) How about the mother's dress? (oilcloth—you might want to bring in a sample of a similar material) Let children tell their own snowy (or sunny or rainy or foggy) day stories and illustrate them with collage.

Materials

* newspaper
* assorted collage materials (such as paper of various textures, foil, cotton balls, string, paper towel tubes, candy wrappers, ribbon, pebbles, shells)
* cardboard, heavy fabric, construction paper (for background)
* white glue
* paint and paintbrushes
* toothbrushes (for spattering paint)

[**TIP**] *Invite families to send in collage materials on a regular basis to keep your art center well stocked. To manage materials, have children use trays (or shoe-box lids) for gathering and storing materials.*

1 Have children cover work areas with newspaper and gather materials for their collages. Encourage them to think about their color schemes and create a palette with their materials, grouping color families together.

2 Let children choose a background to work on. Encourage them to try out some of their colors on different backgrounds to see what works best.

3 Children can arrange materials on their backgrounds a little at a time, gluing them in place when they're satisfied with the look, then adding paint if they wish.

Mix equal parts flour and salt with enough water to make a thick paste. Use to attach heavier objects or to add texture.

LANGUAGE ARTS LINKS

Book Talk

Peter vividly expresses the wonder children feel for the world around them. Whether it's snow falling, a squirrel scampering up a tree, or the sun shining, children are curious about what they see outside their windows and have a natural desire to know more. Use the following questions to guide children in a brief discussion about Peter, the world outside his window, and the world outside their windows.

※ Where do you think the story takes place? What are some clues?

※ What are some ways you are like Peter?

※ Do you remember waking up to a snowy world outside your window? What was it like? What did you do?

※ Why do you think the snowball in Peter's pocket wasn't there when he checked before bed? Can you think of a way to save a snowball?

※ What do you wonder about the world outside your window?

Writer's Corner: Zooming In on the Outside

Make viewfinders to zoom in on the world outside. Have each student fold an index card in half and cut a small square (about one inch) out of the center. Let children decorate their viewfinders, then look through them. Ask children to illustrate something special they see, using collage if they like. (See An Art Lesson, page 41.) Have them write sentences to go with their pictures. To make window frames for students' pictures, follow these steps.

※ Fold construction paper in half and cut out the center, leaving about an inch all the way around.

※ Open the frame and paste the picture to the back.

※ Glue or staple strips of fabric or colorful paper to each side to make curtains.

STORY EXTENSIONS

Movement/Science: Track Makers

Introduce this animal-track activity by letting children take turns making tracks like Peter did in the story. Cut out track shapes (as pictured in the story) and tape them in place on the floor. As you reread that section of the story, let children take turns walking like Peter, "with his toes pointing out…pointing in…. Then he dragged his feet s-l-o-w-l-y to make tracks." If you've got snow outside, let children make their own tracks (or let them get their feet wet and make tracks on dry pavement). Students can start patterns and let classmates continue them.

Explain that animals walk in patterns, too. Some animals, like squirrels, are hoppers. Some, like house cats and deer, are straight walkers. Some, like raccoons and bears, are waddlers. Pass out the Track Makers journal page (see page 45), clear some space, and let children try to move like straight walkers, hoppers, and waddlers. Then have children complete the page to show the tracks they make!

Movement: It's Snowing Students!

Wet snow, fluffy snow, swirly snow, icy snow—there are lots of kinds of snow! The snow in the story is good for making snowballs. What do students think it feels like? (probably wet, not fluffy) Let students pantomime different kinds of snow falling. For example, ask them to fall like the snow in *The Snowy Day*—wet flakes that stick together. Then try soft, fluffy flakes; icy snow; and so on.

43

Science: Snowball Meltdown

If you've got snow on hand, let students scoop some up to make snowballs. Then see how long they last in the classroom under different conditions. Have children measure the amount of snow they use so that each snowball is the same size. Set each snowball in a dish or pan to catch the drips, then place them around the room (on a sunny windowsill; in a closet; under a cover; in the pocket of a spare pair of pants, like Peter did in the story). Place paper and pen next to each snowball and ask students to record observations every 30 minutes. Which snowball do students predict will last longest? Which will melt first?

Language Arts/Science: Pocket Chart Sequence Stories

Call children's attention to the steps Peter takes when getting dressed to go outside in the snow. Ask children to close their eyes and think through the steps they go through to get dressed for different types of weather. Prepare and place the following sentence strips into your pocket chart. (Tip: Use a contrasting-colored marker for the title strip and the underlined prepositions.)

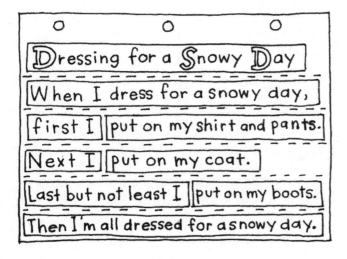

Trim a supply of blank sentence strips to fit in the blank spaces. Help children each compose a set of sentence endings to complete the story. Then have children take turns presenting their sequential stories to the group. Go further by printing each of the lines on a separate mitten-shaped page of copy paper. Reproduce a class set, and have children use the pages to copy and illustrate their stories. Bind together to make individual sequential books. Vary the activity by changing the title to Dressing for a Rainy Day, A Day at the Beach, and so on.

Name_____ Date _____

Track Makers

Can you find ways to use your arms and legs to make tracks like these animals?

hopper

straight walker

waddler

Draw a picture of tracks you can make with your feet.

Are your tracks more like a squirrel's (hopper), a cat's (straight walker), or a bear's (waddler)? _____

Arrow to the Sun: A Pueblo Indian Tale

"Perhaps you are my son," the Lord replied, "perhaps you are not. You must prove yourself. You must pass through the four chambers of ceremony— the Kiva of Lions, the Kiva of Serpents, the Kiva of Bees, and the Kiva of Lightning."
—FROM *ARROW TO THE SUN*

WRITTEN AND ILLUSTRATED BY
GERALD McDERMOTT
(VIKING, 1974)

Pulsating colors and bold geometric shapes rivet children to each page of this hero quest story, a retelling of an ancient Pueblo legend. While children may be unfamiliar with some of the language, they will easily follow the basic structure of the story—and respond to the abstract images with excitement and wonder.

An Inside Look

In his Caldecott acceptance speech, Gerald McDermott comments on the need to nurture children's natural visual perceptions. "Our language is rich and powerful. We strive to learn it, to master it, to put it at our service as a means of communication and expression…Yet we have no such aspirations for the development of our visual sense…" McDermott appeals to those who work with children to "honor art as it opens the human spirit to infinite domains of possibility and fulfillment."

An Art Lesson

Materials

* ⁕ mask-making materials such as paper plates, tagboard, paper grocery bags, and construction paper
* ⁕ scissors
* ⁕ glue
* ⁕ paints, brushes
* ⁕ elastic thread or ribbon

[TIP] *For a thick, glossy paint that won't drip down the paper, mix powdered tempera paint with liquid starch instead of water: Put powder in a jar, add starch, cover, and shake.*

When Gerald McDermott shares *Arrow to the Sun* with young children, they like to pretend that they're invited to the Dance of Life that celebrates the Boy's return to earth. They make abstract masks to wear, using geometric shapes to create representations of themselves. After reading the story the first time, discuss the colors and shapes children see in the masks people wear for the dance. Then let their imagination and inventiveness guide their own mask-making efforts. Reread the story, letting children join in the exuberant dance at the end.

1 Have children choose their mask-making materials. Help them cut out holes to see through. Then let them go to work painting designs, adding geometric shapes, and so on.

2 Use elastic thread or ribbon to fasten paper-plate and tagboard masks. Children who make paper-bag masks can just slip them on.

3 Reread the story. When you get to the last page, invite children to put on their masks and join in!

Building on Books

As with the Boy in *Arrow to the Sun*, the main character in *Raven* (Harcourt Brace & Co., 1993), also by Gerald McDermott and a Caldecott Honor book, takes on different shapes throughout the book—from raven to pine needle to child to raven again. Ask: "How do you know it's Raven each time?" Challenge children to spot the pattern that McDermott repeats as Raven changes shape.

LANGUAGE ARTS LINKS

Book Talk

Use these questions to guide a discussion of the illustrations and how they help tell the story.

❋ As the boy in this story changes to an arrow, back to boy, again to an arrow, and again to a boy, one symbol stays with him. Ask: "How do you know this is still the boy?" Invite children to find this symbol in different scenes—on the boy as a baby, as an older child, and as an arrow. (See Building on Books, page 47, to see how McDermott uses the same technique in retelling another myth.)

❋ What are some shapes that show how people in the story feel? In particular, notice how the shapes the illustrator uses for eyes and mouths change when the characters are sad, when they are celebrating, and so on.

Writer's Corner: Hero Tales

Many children will be familiar with the hero quest theme of *Arrow to the Sun*. For example, some may compare it to modern-day retellings of the story of Hercules. *Saint George and the Dragon* (see page 74) is another fine example. In stories like these, a task is set by someone the main character must please. The tasks, of course, are virtually impossible for an ordinary mortal to attain. But through plenty of courage, inexhaustible strength, and some amount of cleverness, the character is victorious and gets the reward.

Let children rewrite the story of *Arrow to the Sun*, following the hero quest story structure but substituting their own tasks and rewards. In preparation for writing, have children make story maps, identifying the problem, the main events, and how the story ends.

Word Watch: Meaningful Substitutions

**chambers of ceremony
kiva**

After reading, take another look at passages with unusual language. For example, reread the passage quoted on page 46 of this book. Ask: "What do you think a chamber is? A kiva?" Let children look at the pages in the book that show chambers and kivas. Guide them to understand that a *chamber* is like a small room. A *kiva* is an underground chamber, used for Pueblo ceremonies or meetings. What words would children substitute for *chamber* and *kiva* if they were retelling the story? Let them repeat the sentences, using their words.

STORY EXTENSIONS

Arts/Social Studies: What's in a Name?

In searching for someone to lead him to his father, the Boy goes to Corn Planter, Pot Maker, and Arrow Maker. Ask: "How do you think these people got their names?" Look back at the illustrations to see the connection between their names and the work they do. Then children can choose names for themselves based on something they do well (such as Friend Maker, Bike Rider, Book Reader) and make signs that illustrate their choices. To help them get started, talk about pictures and words on signs—for example, "What kind of place might have a sign with a fancy cake on it?" (a bakery) "What might an artist put on a sign?" (paintbrushes or a painting)

Math: Shapes Tell Stories

Geometry is all around us—it's something young children experience every day, in the blocks they build with, the foods they eat, and more. The art in *Arrow to the Sun* is an example of a way people use geometry in the work they do. Gerald McDermott uses shapes almost exclusively to create the rhythmic illustrations in this book.

Take a close look at one page from the story to see how the author/illustrator puts shapes together. For example, looking at the mother and child early in the story, children can find circles, squares, rectangles, concentric circles, and other shapes. What shapes could students use to represent parts of their own bodies? Ask students to make pictures of themselves using pre-cut circles, rectangles, squares, and triangles.

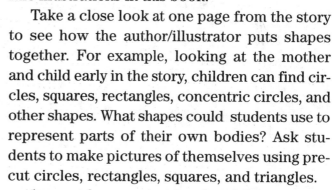

As an at-home extension, let children experiment with arranging shapes to make pictures. Use the templates on page 51 to make pattern blocks. (You can ask children and parents to color and cut them out together.) Ask children to bring the shapes back to school in sandwich bags for further explorations. Eventually, they can glue the pieces in place to make pictures to display.

Music: Sun Celebration

Celebrate the sun by making sun shakers, following these directions.

* Turn two paper plates upside down and decorate the bottoms with sunny designs.

* Stack the plates together and use a hole punch to make holes about an inch apart all the way around.

* Turn one plate right side up and place a handful of dried beans or rice on it.

* Place the other plate on top, right sides together. Use yarn to sew the plates together. Knot the ends of the yarn together.

* Staple yellow and orange streamer rays around the rim of the plates and shake!

Dramatic Play/Social Studies: Adobe Builders

Pueblos, the traditional homes of the Pueblo people, are multilevel buildings constructed from stone or adobe—a building material of sun-dried earth and straw. Let children build a pueblo in the classroom, using large cardboard boxes. (Appliance and computer boxes work well.) Prepare the boxes by cutting entryways in two sides so that children can enter a box from one side and pass through another to a neighboring box. (Save scrap cardboard for other activities; see Dramatic Play, page 100.) Have children arrange the boxes so that one leads into another. Then use sturdy tape to connect them. Let children give the boxes a coat of brown paint. Make sure they understand that boxes on the upper levels are off limits. Then let them make themselves at home!

Shapes Tell Stories

Why Mosquitoes Buzz in People's Ears

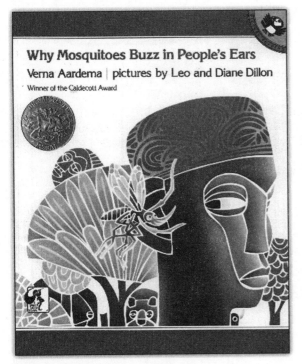

"So, it was the mosquito
who annoyed the iguana,
who frightened the python,
who scared the rabbit,
who startled the crow,
who alarmed the monkey,
who killed the owlet—
and now Mother Owl won't wake the sun
so that the day can come."

—FROM WHY MOSQUITOES BUZZ IN
PEOPLE'S EARS

RETOLD BY VERNA AARDEMA
ILLUSTRATED BY LEO AND DIANE DILLON
(DIAL, 1975)

Take an African safari—and find out what happens when the animals jump to conclusions about one another, setting off a chain reaction that ends in disaster. This story is a perfect introduction to cause and effect. Children will enjoy chiming in on animal sounds and on the repetitive lines, too.

An Inside Look

Leo and Diane Dillon combine their talents to create a sort of third artist. In *Meet the Authors and Illustrators: Volume One*, Diane Dillon says, "...one inspires the other and triggers new thoughts, new directions."

For *Why Mosquitoes Buzz in People's Ears*, the two were concerned about the animals' expressions. In their Caldecott acceptance speech, they explained, "We wanted to indicate human emotions that children could identify with yet retain each animal's distinct features...the most difficult part was trying to put expression onto a mosquito's face." Together, the expressions they capture bring the animals and this story to life.

An Art Lesson: Stenciled Snakes

Materials

* heavy paper
* pencils, paints, old paint brushes
* rubber cement, drafting tape, or white crayons
* pushpins

CAUTION: *If you use rubber cement, be sure to work in an area with plenty of ventilation.*

The illustrations in *Why Mosquitoes Buzz in People's Ears* are mesmerizing—with colors and patterns that make the pictures seem to move. Use the art in this book to introduce *frisket*—the stencil-like technique used by the illustrators. For example, on pages 8 and 9 you'll see a brightly patterned snake slithering into the rabbit's hole. Have students point out the white in the snake's pattern. Explain that this is where the illustrators painted something called masking fluid on the paper. When they added colors, the areas covered with masking fluid remained white.

Though masking fluid is not recommended for use with children, they can achieve similar results with rubber cement or drafting tape. (Available at art stores, drafting tape will peel off paper without tearing it.) For an eye-catching display, try this technique to create a jungle full of snakes in your classroom!

1 Have children draw snake shapes on paper, lightly penciling in patterns.

2 Using old brushes, have children paint rubber cement on their snakes in those areas they want to resist paint. If they're using drafting tape, have them apply it to those areas. (You can also have children experiment with crayon-resist, using a white crayon to fill in areas where they don't want the paint to adhere.)

3 When the rubber cement is dry, let children paint their snakes. When the paint is dry, have them rub off the rubber cement. To build up color in some areas but not others, students can repeat the process, masking areas where they want to retain the base color.

4 Use the snakes to create a colorful display. To add an interactive language arts component, let children add words to the display according to some criteria, such as words that start with the same consonant blend as *snake* (such as *snail, sniffle,* and *snow*); words about snakes (such as *slither, coil, crawl*); or names of different kinds of snakes (*python, anaconda, cobra*).

LANGUAGE LINKS

Book Talk

Focus a discussion on themes from the story that children can relate to their own lives. Guide students in recognizing cause and effect.

- ⁂ What happens when the grumpy iguana goes lumbering off with sticks stuck in his ears?

- ⁂ How does one misunderstanding become a big problem?

- ⁂ What do you learn about the lion from the way he handled the problem?

- ⁂ Have you and a friend ever had a misunderstanding? What happened?

Demonstrate how easily misunderstandings happen by playing a game of telephone. Gather children in a circle and whisper a sentence to the child on your left or right. Have that child whisper the sentence to the next child. Continue until the sentence goes all the way around. Have the last child say the sentence aloud. Share the original sentence and talk about what happened.

Retelling the Tale

Students create delightful stuffed animals to use as props in a retelling of the story.

Materials

- ⁂ craft paper
- ⁂ paints and paintbrushes
- ⁂ markers and crayons
- ⁂ scissors
- ⁂ various arts and craft supplies such as wiggly eyes, yarn, feathers
- ⁂ stapler (or hole punch and yarn)
- ⁂ newspaper

1 Invite children to take another look at the illustrations and name the animals in the story (lion, mosquito, iguana, python, rabbit, crow, monkey, owlets, owl, giraffe, antelope, and so on).

2 Ask each child to choose a different animal to create and paint or color a big picture of it on craft paper that has been folded in half. Let children use craft supplies to decorate their animals.

3 Have children cut out their animals. Then help them

Word Watch: Animal Sounds

mek mek mek mek

wasawusu wasawusu

krik krik krik

kaa kaa kaa

nge nge nge

Children will have fun playing with the unusual sound words in this story, chiming in as you reread it. (Try using different rhythm instruments to accompany each sound.) After reading, write the sound words on chart paper. Talk about how the sounds and animals go together. Ask: "Does *mek mek mek* sound like a grumpy iguana? *Wasawusu wasawusu* like a snake heading into a rabbit hole?" Continue with the other sounds in the story, then invite children to suggest new animal sound words. Add to the chart and display.

staple or sew the two pieces together almost all the way around. (Punch holes around the edges and provide yarn for sewing.)

4 Show children how to stuff their animals with newspaper and close up the opening.

5 Review the sequence of the story. Then let children work together to perform it as a play with their animals.

Building on Books

Team *Why Mosquitoes Buzz in People's Ears* with *A Story A Story* (Atheneum, 1970; 1972 Caldecott medal), an African tale retold and illustrated by Gail E. Haley. Invite children to notice the use of repeated words in both books. In her introduction, Haley explains, "Africans repeat words to make them stronger. For example, 'So small, so small, so small,' means very, very, very small." Use a Venn diagram to record other comparisons.

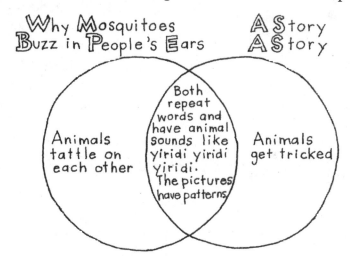

Why Mosquitoes Buzz in People's Ears / A Story A Story

Animals tattle on each other

Both repeat words and have animal sounds like yiridi yiridi yiridi. The pictures have patterns

Animals get tricked

Writer's Corner: Postcard Stories

Greetings from Africa

Have children research to learn more about Africa. Then suggest they write postcard stories about a favorite part. (See template, page 16.) For example, a student might create a set of postcards that picture different animals from Africa. The messages on these postcards can tell more about the animals—for example, where they can be found and what's special about their home. Make sure that students include all of the elements of a postcard: the picture, picture description, stamp, address, and message. If you have a message center, encourage students to "mail" their postcards to classmates.

STORY EXTENSIONS

Movement: Lumber and Leap, Scurry and Slither

Leo and Diane Dillon's jungle is alive with animals. Let children pantomine the movements—slithering like the snake, lumbering like the iguana, and so on. For a change of pace, don't just walk on your way to lunch—choose an animal from the story and let children move down the hall like that animal.

Social Studies/Art: Shape Transformations

This was a map of Africa.

Now it's a part of my giraffe.

Many young children are intrigued by Africa, where the story *Why Mosquitoes Buzz in People's Ears* originates. Let them get to know the shape of this great continent through an activity that encourages creative thinking. Start by giving each child a copy of an outline of Africa. (See page 57.) Ask children to cut out the shape and use it to create something else—for example, tipping it on its side to become the head of a giraffe. Display finished art to help children appreciate differences in creative expression.

Science/Language Arts: Baby Animal Book

Polar Bear Cub

I live in a den under the Arctic snow. In the spring my mother will take me outside.

Do students remember the name for the baby owls in the story? (owlets) What other baby animal names do they know? (for example, cub, kitten, joey, calf) Let each student choose a baby animal to research and report on in baby-book format.

In preparation for this project, you might send a note home requesting that parents who have baby books of their children send them in to share with the class. Talk about the kinds of information parents record in baby books. Suggest that students select four or five pieces of information to include in their books, such as:

☀ a first "photo" of the baby

☀ the baby's home

☀ favorite first foods

☀ favorite ways to play

☀ changes in the first few weeks

A Map of Africa

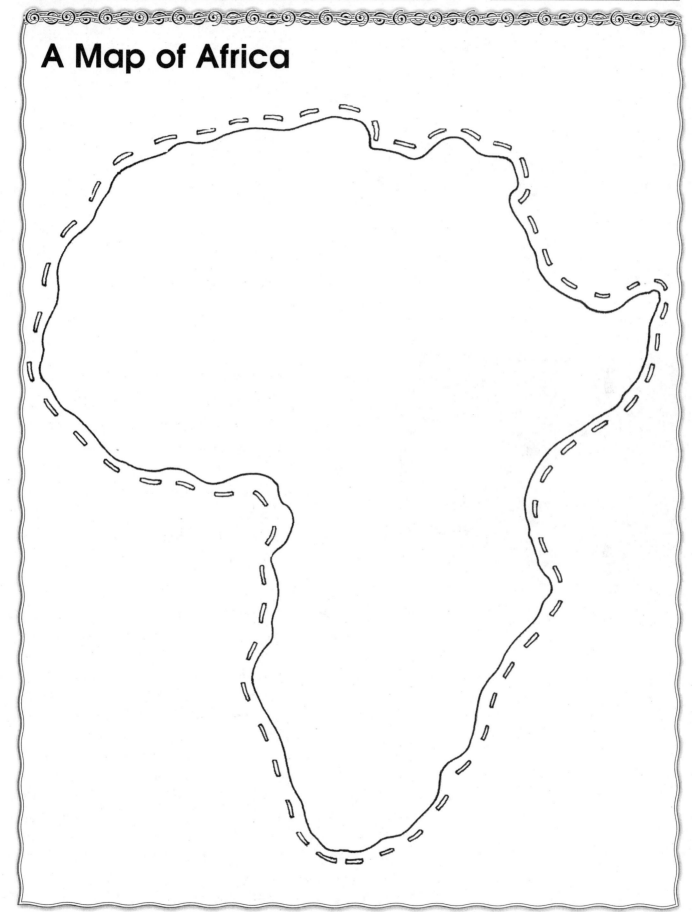

Ox-Cart Man

WRITTEN BY DONALD HALL
ILLUSTRATED BY BARBARA COONEY
(VIKING, 1979)

Journey to the Portsmouth Market of long ago with a farmer whose cart is filled with all the things his family has produced over the year. After he sells everything, he returns home, where the cycle of stitching, carving, candle making, maple-tree tapping, sheep shearing, planting, and other tasks begins again.

In October he backed his ox into his cart and he and his family filled it up with everything they made or grew all year long that was left over.
—FROM *OX-CART MAN*

An Inside Look

Ox-Cart Man is Barbara Cooney's second Caldecott winner. *Chanticleer and the Fox* (Crowell, 1958) was her first. In her Caldecott acceptance speech, Cooney talked about researching an authentic background for the story, set in New Hampshire. First, she needed to establish the time of the story—1832—a time "when the turnpikes were busy... when the brick market building in Portsmouth was standing, and when beards were in fashion." (She wanted the farmer to have a red beard like one of the carpenters who was working on her house at the time.) In paintings that resemble the Early American technique of painting on wood, Cooney captures the changing colors of the New England seasons—from the tans and grays of November to the spring greens of April and May.

An Art Lesson

Materials

* paper and pencils
* assorted pieces of wood (ask a lumberyard to donate scraps)
* tempera paint
* paintbrushes

Explain that the illustrations in *Ox-Cart Man* were created to resemble the Early American technique of painting on wood. Chairs, chests, and floors are just some of the things people painted pictures on. Invite students to take a close-up look at the pictures in the book. Ask: "What do you think makes them look as though they're painted on wood?" (for example, the grainy effect in some of them) Then let children try painting on wood themselves, using an illustration from *Ox-Cart Man* for inspiration or painting scenes of their own.

1 Have children sketch their designs on paper.

2 Before they apply paint to their wood, let children take turns experimenting on an extra piece of wood. For example, how does painting with the grain compare with painting against the grain? What effects can they achieve using a small amount of paint on the brush? What happens when they use more?

3 Let students paint their own wood, let dry, and display.

LANGUAGE ARTS LINKS

Book Talk

Introduce the story by sharing the quote on page 58. Ask: "What do you think the family made or grew all year? Why do you think they're putting it all in the cart?" After reading, invite children to compare family life then and now. You might ask:

* What are some of the things that let you know this story takes place in a different time?

* How do lives pictured in the book differ from your own? (Guide students in discussing differences in travel, in the way we buy things, in the jobs men and women do, and so on.)

* What things are the same? (Help students recognize that people in families still need to help out, someone still needs to make the things we buy, and so on.)

* What questions would you ask the ox-cart man and his family?

Word Watch: A Cartful of Synonyms

coins	**kettle**	**cart**	**shear**
carve	**slits**	**village**	

Use words in this story to explore synonyms. Write the words listed here on wagon-shaped pieces of paper. (Add other words from the story as you wish.) Provide paper cut in other shapes that relate to the story, such as apples. Invite children to suggest synonyms for each word, write them on the apples, then fill the carts!

Building on Books

Ox-Cart Man is the cyclical story of an early nineteenth century family's life through the seasons. Inspire students to think about their own family histories by taking a look at other books with a similar theme. Suggested titles include:

※ *Miss Rumphius* by Barbara Cooney (Viking, 1982)

※ *Yonder* by Tony Johnston (Dial, 1988)

※ *Island Boy* by Barbara Cooney (Viking, 1988)

※ *When I Was Young in the Mountains* by Cynthia Rylant (Dutton, 1982)

Get started by letting small groups of students each select a book to read and discuss. Bring students together to share their thoughts about the stories. Follow up by letting students write their own family history stories, focusing on the recent history of their childhood or interviewing parents or grandparents about life back when.

Writer's Corner: Seasonal Story Wheels

Explore the cyclical structure of this story, reviewing what the family does in each season (making candles in winter, boiling sap for maple syrup in spring, and so on). Then guide students in making story wheels that reflect their family's activities from one season to the next. With a turn of the wheel, they'll be able to read their stories one season at a time.

※ Use a paper plate as a template to trace and cut out two circles from construction paper.

※ Use a pencil to poke a hole through the center of both circles.

❋ Draw lines to divide one circle into four equal parts. Illustrate how you help your family or someone you know as the seasons change, one scene/season per section. Use words too, if you like.

❋ Cut out a window in the front of the second piece of construction paper, as shown, so that when you attach the wheel, a complete section will show through. (You may want to precut windows for students.)

❋ Use a paper fastener to connect the wheels, placing the one with pictures behind the other.

❋ To read your story, turn the wheel. What's happening in each season?

STORY EXTENSIONS

Math/Social Studies: What a Walk!

In the story, we learn that the ox-cart man walked 10 days to get to the market. Talk about how long 10 days is. (For example, students might say it's the same as two weeks of school.) How many days do students think the entire trip lasted? (They'll need to decide whether it also took the man 10 days to return home.) Keep track on a number line. Share peppermint candy when the father gets back to the farm!

Go further by estimating and then calculating how far the father probably walked to the market and back. One way to calculate the distance is to mark off 1/4 mile (1,320 feet) on the playground. (You might have to go back and forth over a shorter distance.) Time children as they walk this distance. Then use that number to calculate how far they could walk in one hour. Use that number to calculate how far they could walk in a day. (There may be factors to fill in, such as stopping for breaks and lunch.) When you've got the mileage, use a map and work backward from Portsmouth to find places the father might have traveled from. Ask: "How might people travel that distance now?"

Social Studies: Where Does Food Come From?

Introduce students to the concept of *resources*. Ask: "How did the family use sheep to make the things they needed?" (They sheared the sheep to get wool to spin to make yarn to knit shawls and mittens.) "How did they use other things to make or get what they needed?" Explain that these things (sheep, trees, flax, and so on) are resources—they provide the family with something they need. Talk about local resources. Ask: "What things do we eat or use that come from our area?" Draw an outline of your state on a large sheet of paper. Let children draw or cut out pictures that show resources from their state, placing them on the map.

Science/Math: Sugar on Snow

Maple sugar from the trees the family tapped is one of the things the ox-cart man packs to sell at the market. Sugar on snow is another traditional maple treat. Make some to share when you read this story and explore changes in states of matter at the same time.

Materials

* maple syrup (about a pint)
* plate
* stove or hot plate
* pot
* spoon
* small paper cups
* snow or crushed ice
* journal page (see page 63)

1 Pour a spoonful of syrup on a plate. Let students tip the plate and describe what they see on their journal pages. Let them touch, smell, and taste the syrup and record observations.

2 While students are at lunch or a special activity, boil the maple syrup until it forms a ball when you drop a bit in cold water.

3 Explain that while they were out, you cooked the syrup. Being careful not to let students touch the pan or the hot syrup, ask: "How does the syrup look now?" Drizzle maple syrup on top of a cup of clean snow or crushed ice. Ask: "What changes do you see?" (It hardens on the snow.) Ask: "Why do you think this happens?" (Heat causes water in the syrup to evaporate, making it thicker. The cold snow makes it harden.)

4 Drizzle maple syrup on cups of snow for children to taste. Follow up with a fun survey: "What is your favorite thing to put maple syrup on?" Graph results. Then extend the survey to the school, posting a graph in the hall and letting passersby register their votes.

JOURNAL PAGE

Sugar on Snow

1. Describe the maple syrup.

   • How does it look?_____

   • How does it feel?_____

   • How does it smell?_____

   • How does it taste?_____

2. How does cooking the maple syrup change it?

   _____

3. What happens when you put the maple syrup on something cold?

   _____

4. Draw a picture of something
   that is like maple syrup.
   Write about how the two
   things are alike.

   _____

   _____

Fables

Wishes, on their way to coming true, will not be rushed.

—FROM *FABLES*

WRITTEN AND ILLUSTRATED BY
ARNOLD LOBEL (HARPERCOLLINS, 1980)

A tree with furry toes, a camel in a tutu, a pig sprouting wings of spun sugar—these are just a few of the characters that star in this collection of fanciful fables, full of wit and gentle lessons to learn. From the author of the well-loved *Frog and Toad* series, these original stories, just a page a piece, are just right for those times when you want to sneak in a quick story.

An Inside Look

Arnold Lobel's Caldecott acceptance speech is full of warmth and good humor—just like his collection of original fables. Lobel shared the struggle that led to this award-winner, a story that is sure to inspire your students when they're stuck getting started. After agreeing to write and illustrate a collection of Aesop's fables for his publisher, Lobel decided these fables were not for him. "I found dogs tearing sheep into pieces…snakes strangling ravens…deer being chewed to bits by lions…it was a far cry from *Frog and Toad*." He gave the bad news to his editor (Charlotte Zolotow) and offered instead to write fables of his own. Still, months went by until finally, confined by a broken bone, he started to write. He began by listing all of his favorite animals. (Traditionally, fables feature animals.) Pictures and stories followed naturally this time.

An Art Lesson

Children can work in groups to make stick puppets of characters from the story. Let them add simple backdrops and act out favorite fables.

1 Together, review the fables, writing titles and character names on the board.

2 Let children team up and choose a fable to perform. Have them start by drawing the main characters on tagboard (one character per piece of tagboard) and decorating them. Have children tape their drawings to sticks to make puppets.

3 Review the setting of each group's fable. For example, "The Ducks and the Fox" takes place outdoors, with the ducks waddling down a tree-lined road toward a pond. Have children make backdrops for their puppet shows on large pieces of cardboard or craft paper. Encourage them to be creative in their designs. The trees for "The Ducks and the Fox" can be three-dimensional, with leaves made from scrunched up paper. Walls for "The Pelican and the Crane," "The Elephant and His Son," and "The Crocodile in the Bedroom" can be created by gluing wallpaper scraps to cardboard or by stamping a repeating design on craft paper.

4 Reread the fables with each group. Then let children practice and perform them as puppet shows.

Materials

* tagboard (precut into approximately 8-by-10 inch pieces)
* markers
* assorted arts and craft supplies such as wallpaper and fabric scraps, wiggly eyes, craft feathers, fake fur scraps
* glue
* rulers, craft sticks, or dowels
* tape
* cardboard, craft paper

[TIP] *These witty fables will make show-stopping performances—the stories are short (making them easy to remember), have plenty of dialogue (making it easy to tell who says what), and are full of fun! To help children get the most out of the experience, line up adult volunteers to work with each group over a period of a week. (For tips on acting out stories, see page 10.)*

LANGUAGE ARTS LINKS

Book Talk

Fables date back to early times, but their messages still have meaning in everyday life. Arnold Lobel's originals are especially easy to connect with. With morals that remind us to be ourselves, to have patience, to persevere, and more, these fables teach life's lessons with plenty of humor. Try these suggestions to explore the structure and meaning of fables.

* ☀ Ask: "What do you notice about the fables we're reading?" (For example, they are all animal stories.)

* ☀ Leave off the moral at the end and invite children to tell what they think each story teaches. (They may come up with more than one idea.) Record their responses and guide them to recognize that fables are stories that teach lessons.

* ☀ Ask: "Can you think of a time you felt like one of the animals in the story? What did you learn?"

Building on Books

Arnold Lobel's *Frog and Toad* books are perennial favorites. Plan a day to celebrate their author, who has written and/or illustrated more than 60 books for children. Encourage children to offer celebration suggestions, too.

* ☀ Create invitations to a Frog and Toad Day, featuring favorite characters from Arnold Lobel stories (or morals from *Fables*).

* ☀ Invite children to bring in their own *Frog and Toad* stories, along with other books by Lobel. Create a display with the books. Include biographical information on the author/illustrator as well.

* ☀ Invite guests to read aloud their favorite stories by the author/illustrator.

* ☀ Let a group of children act out "The Pelican and the Crane." (Crane invites Pelican for tea and cookies. Pelican makes a mess, wiping his mouth with the tablecloth before he leaves. He wonders why no one ever calls him.) Serve tea and cookies to your guests too! (For more performance ideas, see An Art Lesson, page 65.)

Writer's Corner: Favorite Fables

What lessons have children learned in their own lives that they can share with others? Using Arnold Lobel's fables as a model, have children choose their favorite animals to star in original fables. Tips to share as students prepare to write include:

☀ First, tell your story to a friend. Then write it down as you told it.

☀ Use quotation marks to show what each person in your story says. Check the speaker-tag chart (see Word Watch) for words that show how a speaker is talking.

☀ Write the moral at the beginning or the end of your story.

Turn children's stories into a class book. Using the design in *Fables* as inspiration, create borders on pages to frame illustrations and stories. Let children paste their work on the pages. Add front and back covers, then bind.

Three Friends

Once upon a time there lived three friends. One knew how to fly but the other two didn't. They wanted to go to the wizard of flying so that they could all fly.
"But I don't know where to go," said the bluebird.
"Let's go try the bridge," said the cat in a prowly voice.
They started to go across. The smallest one went first. She said, "It's too high off the ground!"
The kitten gave it a try. "I think I can make it." But her paw slipped because the bridge had water on it.
"Help, help," said the kitten and the squirrel. "We might get hurt!"
Everyone was feeling bad and sad. "If we can't get across the bridge, then we won't get to the wizard then we won't get to fly."
"If we can't get across the bridge," said the kitten "then we will have to swim across the river." So they went to the river. They found sticks and a board and they made a bridge to go across.
"We made it," said the kitten. And they got to the wizard.
Things that start bad can end good.

by tucker and Kate.

A Bucket of Brussel Sprouts

No ordinary portions will do for the hippopotamus in "The Hippopotamus at Dinner," who orders "a bathtub of bean soup, a bucket of Brussel sprouts, and a mountain of mashed potatoes." Encourage playfulness with words by making a menu any hippo would love. Start by letting children list foods they would order at a restaurant. Then let them suggest portions for a hippo-size appetite. How about a planeload of pizza and a river of root beer for starters? Have children record and illustrate ideas. Display on the wall, in fast-food menu style.

STORY EXTENSIONS

Art: Picture a Feast

What's your students' idea of the perfect meal? In "The Cat in His Visions," a cat has a "glorious vision" of a meal: "a large, fat fish on a china plate, resting in an ocean of lemon juice and butter sauce." Pass out paper plates and let children draw (or cut out and paste) pictures of favorite meals. Paste plates to large sheets of construction paper and have children add descriptions of their "glorious visions."

Movement: Ballet Dancers and Dreams

Can a camel dance? In *Fables*, a camel dreams of becoming a ballet dancer. "'To make every movement a thing of grace and beauty,' said the Camel. 'That is my one and only desire.'" So, the camel practices pirouettes, relevés, and arabesques—each a hundred times a day! Though her camel friends don't appreciate her talent, she takes great pleasure in her accomplishments, which is all that matters. Invite a local ballet teacher or student to teach a basic routine to students. Practice, then put on a recital as part of a retelling of the story. Follow up by inviting children to share their dreams. How can they work to accomplish them?

Science: Rainbow Maker

What's really at the end of a rainbow? In "The Frogs at the Rainbow's End," three frogs are convinced they will find gold, diamonds, and pearls. With the simple setup described here, students can discover for themselves what's really at the end of a rainbow—and in between.

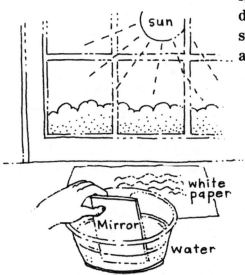

* Fill a clear container with water and set it on a windowsill. Place a sheet of white paper between the container and the window. Show children how to place a small mirror in the water, mirror-side toward the sunlight. Move the mirror until a rainbow appears.

* Let children make rainbows on their own, recording observations on their journal pages. (See page 69.) Do children's drawings indicate that they recognize the pattern of colors in a rainbow? What other discoveries do they make?

Name ________________________ Date ____________

JOURNAL PAGE

Rainbow Maker

Here are pictures of three rainbows I made.

Rainbow 1

Rainbow 2

Rainbow 3

This is something I discovered about rainbows.

____

____

The Glorious Flight: Across the Channel With Louis Blériot

WRITTEN AND ILLUSTRATED BY ALICE AND MARTIN PROVENSEN (PENGUIN, 1983)

Clacketa, Clacketa.

CLACKETA! CLACKETA!

Out of the clouds, right over their heads, soars a great white airship. And a man is sitting in a basket, driving it through the air!

—FROM *THE GLORIOUS FLIGHT*

Take students back in time with this fascinating look at a moment in aviation history. The story tells of Louis Blériot, whose self-built plane sputtered into action at 4:35 A.M. on July 25, 1909, taking him from the coast of France out over the English Channel. Thirty-seven minutes later, he landed in England, making history as the first person to cross water by air.

An Inside Look

In their Caldecott acceptance speech for *The Glorious Flight*, the Provensens said they "wanted to capture for children some of the incredible daring of the first days of flying when men in fragile boxes made of sticks and wire and linen lurched off cow pastures all over the world." Their fascination for planes shines through in their simple but spirited illustrations. From a plane that "flaps like a chicken" to one that "like a great swan…rises into the air" (only to crash into the river), the Provensens capture Louis Blériot's passion, determination, and triumph.

An Art Lesson

As children look at the pictures in *The Glorious Flight*, ask: "What kinds of clues tell you when this story took place?" Talk about the ways details help set the scene for the story. For example, the illustrators needed to know how people dressed during this time, what kinds of transportation existed, what the streets and shops looked like, and so on. Explain that including accurate details makes the story more realistic and believable.

Follow up by inviting children to paint or draw pictures that could be the setting for a story set in their own time and place. Use these questions to guide children in including details that will help them create believable pictures that accurately reflect the time.

1 Clothing: What kinds of clothes do the children wear? The grown-ups?

2 Transportation: In *The Glorious Flight*, the illustrators picture cars and carriages that are true to the time. What methods of transportation represent the ways we travel around town? (Guide children to understand that over time, transportation has changed. To illustrate this point, ask children to compare cars in the story with cars today.)

3 Streets and Shops: The narrow shop-filled streets in *The Glorious Flight* represent those of the early 1900s in a French city. How would children picture the streets where their families shop?

Building on Books

Share *Voyages of Discovery: The Story of Flight* (Scholastic, 1995). Though the text in this book may be too advanced for many young readers, the interactive pages will hold their interest. See-through, fold-out, flap, and other special pages will inspire their creativity. Use the book as a model for students' own interactive books about flight. *How Do Airplanes Fly?* (Scholastic, 1997) offers an on-level look at the science of flight and includes three model airplanes to fly.

LANGUAGE ARTS LINKS

Book Talk

Word Watch: BIG Words

CLACKETA! CLACKETA!

As you reread the story, point out these words to children. (See quote, page 70.) Ask: "Why do you think some of the words are printed in capital letters?" Let them take turns rereading these lines using their voices to make the words "big." Encourage children to recognize that by making the letters big, the authors help us "hear" the loudness of the plane. Ask: "What are other reasons an author might use capital letters for some words?" (for example, to show feelings such as anger and surprise) Encourage children to be on the lookout for "big" words in other stories they read.

Factually accurate, *The Glorious Flight* is also full of fun. The Blériot I "flaps like a chicken." Another plane hops like a rabbit. There are "slight crashes," but Papa holds on to his humor—and his determination. After sharing the story, talk with students about Papa's perseverance. Guide children in making connections between themselves and Papa—and in building the self-esteem that will help them work hard to accomplish their goals.

* Why do you think it took Papa so many tries to build a flying machine that worked?

* What do you think kept Papa from getting discouraged? (Help children recognize his sense of humor as well as other positive traits.)

* How do you think Papa felt when he and his plane landed in England?

* What is something you have worked hard at? What helped you want to try, even though it was hard?

Writer's Corner: The ABCs of Flying

Explore airplanes by making a collaborative ABC book of flight. Start by sharing *Let's Fly from A to Z* by Doug Magee and Robert Newman (Cobblehill, 1992), an ABC book of people, places, and things that have to do with flying. Begin by brainstorming some ideas together. Record suggestions in any order they are offered. (Don't worry at this point if the suggestions are not in ABC order.) Invite each child to choose one letter and create a page in the book for it. Children can use items already recorded or come up with their own.

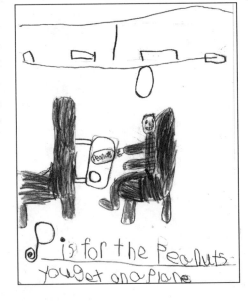

P is for the Peanuts you get on a plane.

STORY EXTENSIONS

Science/Math: Time Line of Flight

Invite your students to learn more about the history of flight by asking them to bring in pictures and models of flying things as well as toy planes, helicopters, and so on. Together, make a time line, placing the pictures and objects in the order students think they were invented. Adjust the time line after researching the items. Which was the first to fly?

Science: Make It Fly!

Explore the science of flight with paper airplanes. Begin by making basic square planes (see illustration below). Have students take turns launching their planes, recording observations on flight logs. Compare flight times with the world record: 18.8 seconds set by Ken Blackburn in 1994.

Follow up by discussing the forces that keep the planes in the air. In *The World Record Paper Airplane Book* (Workman, 1994), Ken Blackburn likens weight and lift to a game of tug-of-war. *Weight* is the downward pull (gravity), *lift* the upward. Air resistance causes *drag*, or a backward pull. *Thrust* pushes a plane forward. (Your arm supplies the thrust for a paper airplane.)

Flight Log

Pilot _____
Copilot _____
Date _____

	Estimated Flight Time	Actual Flight Time	Comments
Test 1			
Test 2			
Test 3			

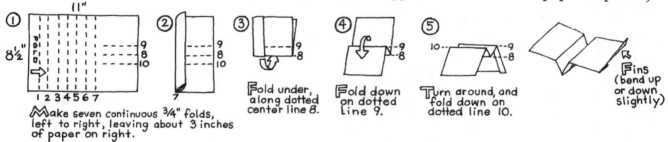

① 11" 8½" [Fold here] 1 2 3 4 5 6 7 Make seven continuous ¾" folds, left to right, leaving about 3 inches of paper on right.

② 9 8 10 7

③ 9 8 Fold under, along dotted center line 8.

④ 9 8 Fold down on dotted Line 9.

⑤ 10 9 8 Turn around, and fold down on dotted line 10.

Fins (bend up or down slightly)

Social Studies: We're Pioneers, Too!

History is filled with pioneers—some known, others (like Blériot) less known. In them, we can see what the pioneering spirit is all about—a sense of adventure, a risk taken.

Take a look at ways students' everyday achievements are like those of Louis Blériot and other history-making pioneers. Ask: "How is trying something new or going someplace you've never been before like being a pioneer?" Invite children to draw pictures of or write about milestones that represent their pioneer spirit—such as reading a book for the first time. Create a display featuring your young pioneers' firsts.

Saint George and the Dragon

RETOLD BY MARGARET HODGES
ILLUSTRATED BY TRINA SCHART HYMAN
(LITTLE, BROWN, 1985)

There's something about dragons that will always appeal to children— and the "great hill" of a dragon in this story, described in delicious detail, is no exception. But as in any great hero quest story, there's a knight waiting to do battle—to save the people from the dreadful dragon and win the princess (with the kingdom thrown in, too). Based on Edmund Spenser's *Faerie Queen*, this retelling will leave your students spellbound.

The dreadful dragon lay stretched on the sunny side of a great hill, like a great hill himself...
—FROM *SAINT GEORGE AND THE DRAGON*

An Inside Look

Instead of sketching ideas for stories she's illustrating, Trina Schart Hyman thinks about them, asking herself questions about the characters and the landscape. In her Caldecott acceptance speech, she said, "I think about the characters and what makes them tick and where they're coming from and where they might be going to. Who *are* these people? What do they like to eat for breakfast?" She dreams about them, too. "When my dreams start to become the dreams of the characters in the book...then I know what to do with my pictures."

An Art Lesson

Materials

☀ ruler

☀ white paper

☀ pencils

☀ black pens or crayons

☀ watercolor paints or colored pencils

☀ paintbrushes

☀ gold and silver crayons, paint, or markers

Flowering vines, seascapes, dragons, and other elaborate designs decorate the pages in *Saint George and the Dragon* in the style of an illuminated manuscript. Here's how your students can make similarly dazzling designs, perfect for illustrating their own medieval tales (or any other story).

1 Use a ruler to mark borders of an inch or two around the edges of white paper. Have children copy their stories onto this paper, leaving off the first letter of the first word.

2 Have children use pencil to write the first letter, making it big and fancy, then outline it with black crayon or pen. Let children use watercolors to paint designs on their fancy letters. (Crayons or colored pencils will work too.)

3 Take another look at border designs in *Saint George and the Dragon*. Then have children paint or color their own borders, incorporating miniature drawings of dragons, princesses, and other characters in their stories if they want.

4 For a special touch, let children add a bit of gold or silver paint to their designs.

Building on Books

What does a dragon really look like? Students will discover the surprising answer in *Everyone Knows What a Dragon Looks Like* by Jay Williams (Four Winds, 1976). Richly illustrated by Mercer Mayer, this story tells of a city in trouble, and the unlikely dragon who comes to the rescue. The trouble is, everyone is so sure that they know what a dragon looks like, they refuse to let the little old man, who is, in fact, a dragon, help.

LANGUAGE ARTS LINKS

Book Talk

Students will have no trouble recognizing the conflict in *Saint George and the Dragon*. For three days, a brave knight and a monstrous dragon battle. Though dwarfed by the dragon, the knight has courage going for him, as well as magical water from an ancient spring and healing dew from an apple tree. And of course there's the "fair and faithful" Una to encourage him. Use the following questions to explore conflict, noting each character's strengths and weaknesses.

　※ Why do you think the knight fought the dragon?

　※ Do you think the knight was afraid? Why?

　※ How do you think the knight managed to defeat the dragon?

　※ What other stories do you know that have characters who have conflicts like this?

　※ Have you ever had to do something that was scary? What did you do?

Writer's Corner: Big News!

Children are natural news reporters—they've almost always got a story to tell about something going on around them. Turn your classroom into a newsroom to learn more about writing news stories. Begin by looking at real front-page news together. List parts of stories on a chart, such as headlines, bylines, datelines, quotes, and key events, and display an example of each. Then let your young journalists go to work to write front-page stories about the battle between the dragon and the knight, the ending, or any other part of the story. If students have access to a computer, you might want to have them publish their stories using the newspaper templates in software such as ClarisWorks.

[TIP] *To learn more about using journalism in your writing program, try* Free to Write: A Journalist Teaches Young Writers *by Roy Peter Clark (Heinemann, 1995).*

Word Watch: Alliteration

dreadful dragon
sunny side

Use the story to introduce alliteration. Encourage children to use this technique to play with the language in their own writing.

　※ Read the sentence quoted on page 74. Write it on the board. Ask: "What do you notice about the words in this sentence?" Guide children to recognize words that start with the same consonant sound.

　※ Repeat this procedure with other sentences from the story, asking: "What do you like about the way these words sound?"

　※ Let children write some examples of alliteration from other stories on chart paper and post for inspiration.

STORY EXTENSIONS

Math: How Long Is a Dragon's Tail?

With a tail that "wound in a hundred folds over his scaly back and swept the land behind him for almost half a mile," this dragon is a force to be reckoned with. Let students estimate the length of the dragon's tail, suggesting comparisons—for example, "I think it's as long as our playground." Together, plan a way to show how long the dragon's tail is. For example, measure a hallway and calculate how many placed end-to-end would equal 1/2 mile (2,640 feet; 880 yards; 804.67 meters).

My dragon is strong because he's made of titanium.
James

Art/Science: An Invincible Dragon

Even with its scales of brass, sharp claws, stinger-equipped tail, and fire-breathing mouth, the dragon in *Saint George and the Dragon* didn't stand a chance against the noble knight. What kind of dragon would? List the characteristics of the dragon in the story (brass scales, iron teeth, and so on). Ask: "How would you improve on these to design a dragon that would be invincible?"

Divide the class into small groups to design dragons. Integrate research into the project by investigating materials that would help protect a dragon. For example, students might want to find out what the strongest metal is, what space suits are made of, and so on. Ask groups to diagram their dragons, writing captions to tell what makes them the powerful creatures they are.

Social Studies: Leaders Then and Now

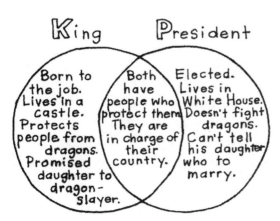

King / President

Born to the job. Lives in a castle. Protects people from dragons. Promised daughter to dragon-slayer.

Both have people who protect them. They are in charge of their country.

Elected. Lives in White House. Doesn't fight dragons. Can't tell his daughter who to marry.

Saint George and the Dragon is set in a time when kings ruled. Use the story to start a discussion about leaders today. Get a sense of what children know by asking, "Who are some leaders you know?" Use a Venn diagram to compare the king to leaders who children are familiar with—for example, the principal of your school or the President of the United States. Guide children in recognizing leadership qualities in others and themselves.

Owl Moon

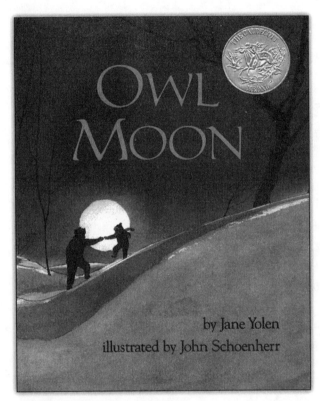

When you go owling
you don't need words
or warm or anything but hope.
That's what Pa says.
The kind of hope that flies
on silent wings under a
shining Owl Moon.
—FROM OWL MOON

WRITTEN BY JANE YOLEN
ILLUSTRATED BY JOHN SCHOENHERR
(PHILOMEL, 1987)

"Whoo-whoo-who-who-who-whoooooo..." The wind is quiet, the moon bright. It's a night for owling. This peaceful and poetic story tells of the special experience a father and young child share on a winter night—and reminds us all of the wonders of the natural world. For the full effect, serve up this story with cups of hot cocoa!

An Inside Look

Jane Yolen dedicated *Owl Moon* to her husband, who took their children owling. Illustrator John Schoenherr also took nighttime walks in the woods with his children, where they too saw owls and other animals. In fact, the farm pictured in *Owl Moon* is the Schoenherr farm; the trails are those he and his family followed. Tucked among the trees and shadows are the animals that make their homes in these woods—a deer resting behind a tree, a raccoon peering out from his hole in a tree, a mouse hiding in the shadows.

An Art Lesson

Materials

❋ drawing paper

❋ pencils

❋ colored pencils

How did John Schoenherr create pictures that make you feel like you're in the woods on a cold night? Not only was the setting for the story right outside his windows at home, but he had years of drawings and photographs to use as reference. Invite students to discover how they can strengthen their own realistic drawings with this exploration.

1 Think of something outside the classroom—maybe a walkway, a cluster of trees, or a flowerpot.

2 Ask students to use their imagination to draw pictures of the scene you describe.

3 When students are finished, take fresh paper and pencils outside and allow them to draw the same scene again— this time studying the actual scene first.

4 Let students compare pictures. How is the second picture different from the first? Which is more realistic?

For students who want to do more with realistic drawings, share *Drawing From Nature* by Jim Arnosky (Lothrop, Lee & Shepard, 1987). From noticing how birds' beaks are joined to their heads to learning how to make trees whose branches reach for the light, this book will inspire children to take a new look at nature.

Building on Books

Evocative watercolors in *Owl Moon* capture the cold of the winter night, the stillness of the woods. Vivid language lets us listen as the father calls out—whoo-whoo-who-who-who-whoooooo— and the echo comes back.

Realistic stories like this often appeal to children who find it easy to place themselves in the story and relate to characters' feelings and experiences, making meaningful connections between the book and their own lives. Organize book groups to explore realistic fiction. (See page 6.) A sampling of favorite realistic children's books follows.

❋ *Mirette on the High Wire* by Emily Arnold McCully (Putnam, 1992) (See page 92.)

❋ *Seven Kisses in a Row* by Patricia MacLachlin (HarperCollins, 1983)

❋ *Stevie* by John Steptoe (HarperCollins, 1969)

❋ *Island Boy* by Barbara Cooney (Viking, 1988)

LANGUAGE ARTS LINKS

Book Talk

After reading, invite students to think about how the words and pictures combine to create the mood in this story.

* Why do you think *Own Moon* is a good title for this story?

* How is the story like a poem?

* Why do you think the father and child are pictured so small in many of the illustrations?

* Why do you think the illustrator filled the page at the end with the owl?

* What are some ways in which the words and illustrations make this story seem real to you?

Follow That Sound

Fine-tune students' listening skills with an owling game. Begin by inviting one student to be the owl. While the others cover their eyes, have the owl hide. Let students take turns calling the owl (whoo-whoo-who-who-who-whooooooo), awaiting its response. Can students follow the sound to locate the owl? For a variation, let one child sit facing away from the others. While one child in the group makes an owl sound, have the child facing away try to guess which classmate is the "owl."

Writer's Corner: Quiet Times Together

"If you go owling you have to be quiet, that's what Pa always says." In *Owl Moon*, both pictures and text help readers feel the quiet of the woods, broken now and then by a train whistle, the crunch of snow, and the sound of a great horned owl.

What special quiet times do your students and their families share? Curling up with a parent and a book? Playing a board game together? Watching the stars at night? Invite each student to share a favorite quiet-time activity (this could be with a parent, older sibling, grandparent, babysitter, and so on). Then have them write about and illustrate it. Encourage children to use words and pictures to create a sense of peacefulness in their stories like that found in *Owl Moon*.

My favorite quiet time is going to the Walking Dunes at Montauk Beach. You can hear the ocean, and you can hear the birds. It makes me feel peaceful as an angel.

Francesca
8 yrs. old

STORY EXTENSIONS

Science/Language Arts: All About Owls

Owls intrigue children, who from an early age love to call out like these creatures. Use this natural interest to inspire a class book. Find a focus by completing a KWL chart, recording what children know (K) and what they want to learn (W). Assign children to groups to research questions. Let them report their findings by creating pages for a class book, using the template on page 82 to make owl-shaped pages. Punch holes above the ears and tie pages together with yarn. Complete the KWL chart by filling in what students learned (L).

Math/Science: Wide Wide Wings

How wide is an owl's wingspan? Research the wingspans of owls and other birds. (For example, the American white pelican has a wingspan of about nine feet, the peregrine falcon about three feet.) Have children cut yarn or string to represent the width of each, (taping labels on strings). Then let them team up to compare the wingspans with their own arm spans. What bird comes closest to a match? Follow up by brainstorming ways to organize the strings (for example, by size order, bigger than my arm span/smaller than my arm span/the same as my arm span, and so on).

Science: Bird-Watching Walk

Take bird-watching walks with your students. First, use a field guide book to research birds that are native to your area. Let students make bird-spotting sheets to bring with them, drawing pictures of the birds and recording descriptive details. As they bird-watch, encourage students to record places they spot the birds, the sounds they make, and so on.

Feed the birds! Hang coconut halves filled with bird seed from a tree. Watch to see who visits. What do they eat?

All About Owls

Song and Dance Man

WRITTEN BY KAREN ACKERMAN
ILLUSTRATED BY STEPHEN GAMMELL
(KNOPF, 1988)

"I wonder if my tap shoes still fit?" Grandpa says with a smile. Then he turns on the light to the attic, and we follow him up the steep, wooden steps.

—FROM *SONG AND DANCE MAN*

Grab your hat and cane and head on up to the attic with Grandpa for a vaudeville show that is "better than any show on TV." For the full effect, paint a large lidded box and stock your "trunk" with old hats, canes, bow ties, and other props for your reading (and for dramatic play after). Gather children around on blankets. Spotlight the area with a lamp as you read.

An Inside Look

Stephen Gammell, the illustrator of such favorites as Caldecott Honor winner *The Relatives Came* (by Cynthia Rylant; Bradbury, 1985), has a style that "sparkle[s] with personality." (*Publishers Weekly*, October 14, 1988) Though he has written several children's books, he says he prefers illustration. "Yes, I have written a few books, but the words are really nothing more than something to keep the art flowing smoothly." (From *Something About the Author*, Vol. 81) Gammell also won a Caldecott Honor for *Where the Buffalos Begin* by Olaf Baker (Frederick Warne, 1981).

An Art Lesson

Materials

❋ colored pencils

❋ drawing paper

[TIP] *To further inspire your young artists, let them make sketchbooks. (Bind plain paper in report covers or with paper fasteners.) Encourage children to sketch the world around them—people, places, and things.*

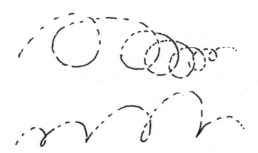

A close look at this book's lively illustrations reveals the ways the illustrator used colored pencil to bring the song and dance man's show to life. You can almost see Grandpa gliding across the floor, hear his toes tap, and watch him spin and jump until at last, out of breath but smiling, the show is over and his grandchildren clap and shout "Hurray!"

Invite children to notice lines in the *Song and Dance Man* illustrations—lines that make shadows, lines that make light, lines that slide, leap, and so on. Encourage them to find their own words to describe lines, too. Then let children experiment with ways they can use lines to bring their own drawings to life.

1 Let children experiment with making different lines—thick and thin, dotted, and dashed, and those that go up, down, around, zigzag, and so on.

2 Ask: "Can you make lines that move the way you do when you do a somersault?" Follow up by suggesting other descriptions such as lines that skip, lines that look like a bouncing ball, lines that jump, and so on.

3 Follow up by letting children add other elements to their lines to create pictures.

Building on Books

Revisit the theme of grandparents with these stories. Add stories children write about their own grandparents, too. (See Tell Me a Story, page 86.)

Now One Foot, Now the Other by Tomie dePaola (Putnam, 1981). A boy whose grandfather helped him take his first steps gives his grandfather the same gentle help after a stroke.

Sophie by Mem Fox (Harcourt Brace, 1997). Explore life's passages with a story about a little girl and grandpa.

When I Was Young in the Mountains by Cynthia Rylant (Dutton, 1982). The author shares memories of growing up with her grandparents in Appalachia—taking trips to the swimming hole, pumping water from the well for baths, and more.

Wilfrid Gordon McDonald Partridge by Mem Fox (Kane/Miller, 1989). When a young boy finds out that his elderly friend has lost her memory, he tries to find it for her.

LANGUAGE ARTS LINKS

Book Talk

Word Watch:
Using Your Senses

dusty brown, leather-trimmed trunk
smell of cedar chips
bright lights twinkle
silvery tap

Reread the story, asking students to notice words that help them picture the attic and Grandpa's show. In particular, notice words with sensory appeal. Can students feel the dusty trunk, smell the cedar chips, see the lights, and hear Grandpa's toes tapping? Invite children to share stories of their own. What sensory words have they used?

Out of an old cedar-scented trunk in the attic come tap shoes, bowler hats, striped vests, bow ties—everything Grandpa needs to take his grandchildren back to his vaudeville days. After reading the story, explore the idea of time with these questions. Be sure to let children share stories of their own favorite activities with grandparents, too. (See Tell Me a Story, page 86, for more.)

* Why do you think Grandpa keeps his song and dance shoes in a trunk in the attic?

* When do you think Grandpa was a song and dance man? What are some clues?

* What do you think the "good old days" are?

Writer's Corner: A Trunkful of Jokes

"Know how to make an elephant float?... One scoop of ice cream, two squirts of soda, and three scoops of elephant!" Jokes are part of Grandpa's vaudeville act and though he tells the same one again and again, he still laughs every time. They're an important part of young children's lives, too. Using riddles, rhymes, and knock-knocks as models, they delight in making up and telling their own jokes—some of them very involved and drawn out. Let children share a few favorites. Then use their natural sense of humor to make a trunkful of jokes to share.

* Cover a rectangular cardboard box and lid with craft paper and decorate.

* Tape the lid to the top of the box along one long side. Slit the two corners of the taped side of the lid to make a hinged top.

* Glue a handle to the lid (ribbon or a strip of fabric will do).

* Invite children to write and illustrate jokes and place them in the box. (You can have them write punch lines upside down on the paper.) Invite children to use the jokes when they plan their own song and dance shows. (See Tapping Toes, page 86.)

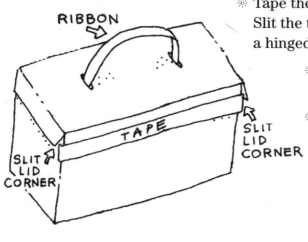

RIBBON

TAPE

SLIT LID CORNER

SLIT LID CORNER

STORY EXTENSIONS

Movement: Tapping Toes

Let students put on their own soft-shoe show. Just tape a penny to the sole of each shoe near the toe. Put on some lively piano music and invite children to try out their tappers! Can they make "soft, slippery sounds like rain on a tin roof" (from *Song and Dance Man*)? What other sounds can they make? As an extension, let children combine their tap-dancing with magic acts, jokes, and songs for vaudeville shows like Grandpa's.

Social Studies: Memory Makers

A time before TV? Young children have a difficult time grasping weeks gone by, much less decades. To expand their understanding of time, make memory trunks.

* Have children decorate shoe boxes and lids to make mini-trunks. For hinged trunk lids, see page 85.

* Ask children to think about their "good old days"—a vacation or trip, a birthday, the day a new pet arrived. Have children choose items that represent their memories and place them in their trunks. Let children take turns opening up their trunks and sharing stories about the items inside.

Social Studies: Tell Me a Story

Have children interview grandparents or older family friends, inviting them to share memories of their past. (You could also visit a senior center for this.) Children can document their interviews with words and pictures or use audiocassettes or videotape if available. Sample interview questions follow.

* Did you have a TV when you were a child? What was your favorite show? What other things did you like to do for fun?

* What were the best things about school when you were a child? What was your least favorite thing?

* What games did you play when you were my age?

* Did you go to movie theaters or other kinds of shows? How much was a show? How much was popcorn?

Lon Po Po: A Red Riding Hood Story From China

WRITTEN AND ILLUSTRATED BY ED YOUNG (PHILOMEL, 1989)

In this Chinese version of "Little Red Riding Hood," three children are tricked into believing that a hungry wolf is their Po Po (grandmother), but together they outsmart him.

An Inside Look

Ed Young's wolf seems to leap off the pages in *Lon Po Po*. How did he bring such life to the illustrations? After researching the story, Young says, "I drew a whole series on how wolves communicate with each other, using their ears, their tails, and the way they hold themselves. That had to be right because the wolf talks to the children in the story, so he has to be alive to them." (From *Meet the Authors and Illustrators, Volume One*)

Once, long ago, there was a woman who lived alone in the country with her three children, Shang, Tao, and Paotze. On the day of their grandmother's birthday, the good mother set off to see her, leaving the three children at home.

Before she left, she said, "Be good while I am away, my heart-loving children; I will not return tonight. Remember to close the door tight at sunset and latch it well."

—FROM *LON PO PO*

An Art Lesson

Materials

* pastels, colored pencils
* watercolors and paintbrushes
* drawing paper
* scissors
* construction paper (larger than the drawing paper)
* paste

Before starting on this art project, let students suggest words that describe Ed Young's dramatic illustrations. *Soft, shadowy,* and *mysterious* are some of the words they might use. Next, invite students to notice the way the illustrations are divided into sections, or panels, on the page. (The illustrator used techniques from Chinese panel art to create this look.) Let children use a simplified version of the illustrator's technique to make their own panel art following these steps.

1 Invite children to use the pastels and watercolors to create scenes from a story on drawing paper. Encourage them to fill the page.

2 Have children cut the illustrations into several strips.

3 Show children how to paste the panels to construction paper, leaving a little space around the top, bottom, and sides of each strip.

LANGUAGE ARTS LINKS

Book Talk

How does *Lon Po Po* compare to other versions of the Red Riding Hood story? (See Building on Books, page 89.) Guide a discussion with questions about character, setting, problem, and solution.

* How is the wolf in *Lon Po Po* like the wolf in the Red Riding Hood story you know? How are they different?
* How are the other characters in the story alike or different?
* Where does the wolf go in *Lon Po Po*? In the other version?
* What does the wolf want to do in each story?
* How do the characters solve the problem in each story?

Take a look at other versions of the Red Riding Hood story. A sampling of titles follows.

Little Red Riding Hood by Trina Schart Hyman (Holiday, 1982). Magnificent illustrations help tell the story of the cunning wolf, Little Red Riding Hood, and her grandmother. (For another look at the illustrator's award-winning style, see *Saint George and the Dragon*, page 74.)

Red Riding Hood by James Marshall (Dial, 1987). In this playful version of the tale, a hunter is on hand to save the day.

Word Watch: Meaningful Substitutions

heart-loving

ginkgo

hei yo

Read the passage quoted on page 87. Check students' understanding of unusual language by asking: "What word could you substitute here for *heart-loving*?" Reread the story, stopping to discuss other unusual language, including:

☀ **Ginkgo:** The children in this story trick the wolf by offering him the fruit of the gingko. "One taste and you will live forever," the eldest child tells him. Ask: "If this story took place where you live, what tree would you use?"

☀ **Hei yo:** Ask: "If you were one of the children in the story, what would you say or sing instead of *hei yo* as you were using all your strength to pull the basket holding the wolf up into the tree?"

Perform a Play

Because many children will be familiar with the story of Red Riding Hood, they will have information to draw on as they write and rehearse a play version. (*Lon Po Po* has a lot of dialogue too, making it easy for children to decide what each character in their play will say.) Begin by sharing *Onstage & Backstage at the Night Owl Theater*, a behind-the-scenes look at a production of Cinderella; see page 10. Next, let children work in teams to handle each part of their production (actors, set designers, playbill producers, and so on). Invite parents and other classes to a performance! (See Act It Out, page 10, for tips on producing plays with children.)

Writer's Corner: Favorite Fairy Tales

In addition to writing and illustrating *Lon Po Po*, Ed Young illustrated *Yeh-Shen: A Cinderella Story From China*, written by Ai-Ling Louie (Philomel, 1982). Unlike the European version children may be familiar with, this story features a magic fish. Use these stories to inspire children's own retellings of favorite fairy tales. Questions to guide their writing follow.

☀ If you're retelling Red Riding Hood, what might Red Riding Hood wear instead of a hood? Where will the wolf go to look for the child (or children)? Might you substitute another creature for the wolf?

☀ If you're retelling Cinderella, who will take the place of the magic fish or the fairy godmother? How will your Cinderella dress? Will she wear glass slippers or stylish sneakers? What if, instead of three sisters, your story had three brothers?

STORY EXTENSIONS

Social Studies: Around the World With Granny

In this story, the children call their granny Po Po. (*Lon Po Po* means Granny Wolf in Chinese.) Invite children to share the names they have for their grandmothers. Learn other words for Grandma too—for example *Oma* (German), *Babcia* (Polish), *Abuela* (Mexican). Locate the origins of these names on a map. Ask: "Why do you think that some of you have different names for your grandmas?"

Art/Math: Near and Far

Perspective plays a big part in the illustrations in *Lon Po Po* and in the mood they create. Reread the story, asking students to pay careful attention to the wolf. In pictures where the wolf looks especially scary, ask: "Is the wolf close up or far away?" Look at the picture of the wolf on the ground with the girls looking down from the tree. Ask: "Does the wolf seem so scary now?"

Continue to explore the concept of perspective with this activity. While one child stands still, have another child move far enough away so that he or she can see the whole person. Ask a volunteer to help you measure this distance. Have the observer move closer and closer to the student standing still. At what distance can the child see only part of the other student? The face? Discuss the concept of near and far and how distance changes the way we see things. Then let children create sets of drawings to show how something or someone looks from far away, then from close up.

Science: Senses at Work

How do wolves hunt? Help children understand the difference between wolves they meet in folktales and those in the wild with an activity that explores how wolves use their senses to find food.

* Have students form groups of three or four. In each group, have one child be a wolf and another be a mouse. Other students will observe, then take a turn as one of the animals when you repeat the activity.

* Find an area where students can spread out (the

cafeteria, gym, or playground) and have groups put a little distance between themselves.

☀ Begin the hunt by blindfolding wolves and asking mice to move away from their groups (about 20 feet).

☀ As wolves cup their hands around their ears (real wolves perk up their ears for this purpose), have the mice squeak. Have wolves listen for the squeak, turning slowly to try to "catch" the sound in their cupped ears. When wolves are ready, have them point in the direction of the squeaks.

☀ Repeat the activity to give everyone a turn as wolf and prey. Follow up by discussing students' observations. Ask: What senses do wolves use to find food? (Hearing, also smell—but that's another experiment!) Why do you think wolves have become endangered?

Building on Books

Learn more about wolves—and the importance of using natural resources wisely—through the eyes of an Indian boy in *The Land of Gray Wolf* by Thomas Locker (Dial, 1991). The boy, Running Deer, tells of white settlers moving in and clearing the forests. Years later, when they've used up the soil, they move on. Trees again begin to cover the land, giving hope that the howl of wolves may one day be heard again. Before sharing the story, record children's impressions of wolves. Do the same after reading, noting any changes to children's impressions. Go further by looking at ways children use resources wisely, such as using recycled paper to conserve trees.

Mirette on the High Wire

WRITTEN AND ILLUSTRATED BY EMILY ARNOLD MCCULLY
(PUTNAM, 1992)

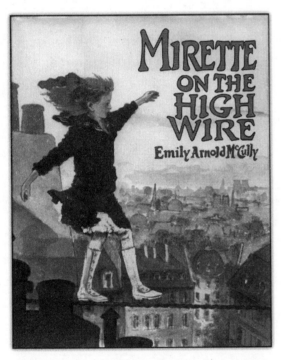

In ten tries she balanced on one foot for a few seconds. In a day, she managed three steps without wavering. Finally, after a week of many, many falls, she walked the length of the wire.

—FROM MIRETTE ON THE HIGH WIRE

"I almost felt like I was there." That's what one young child said about *Mirette on the High Wire*—a response that speaks volumes for this spirited story, set in Paris in the 1890s. Mirette discovers a guest at her mother's boardinghouse "crossing the courtyard on air" and begs him to teach her how to do it. What she doesn't know is that the stranger coaching her is the Great Bellini— a master wire walker for whom fear has put a halt to his high-wire act. When he returns to the high wire, it is Mirette who gives him courage—and they "cross the sky" together.

An Inside Look

The cover of *Mirette on the High Wire* will captivate children—who will be riveted by a young girl poised on the wire, looking out over the city stretched out below. The idea for this book came from the real-life high-wire walker Blondin, with some of the author's own life woven in. Emily Arnold McCully was a daredevil herself as a child, and used her own memories to capture nine-year-old Mirette's spirit.

An Art Lesson

Materials

* craft paper
* yarn
* pushpins
* plain paper
* paints and brushes, markers, crayons
* sequins, glitter glue
* scissors

Let children put themselves on the high wire with this activity.

1 Cover a wall space or bulletin board with craft paper. Tack a length of yarn from one end to the other.

2 On plain paper, children can draw or paint pictures of themselves walking or doing highwire tricks. Have the book handy for artistic inspiration. Let them add sparkle to their scenes with sequins or glitter glue.

3 Ask children to cut around their pictures and tack them to the wire. Let them add dialogue balloons that express messages from the story, such as "I can do anything if I dare to try!"

LANGUAGE ARTS LINKS

Book Talk

Though set in the nineteenth century, children will easily relate to Mirette and her daredevil spirit. Invite their personal response to the story, letting children share their own daring deeds (riding a two-wheeler for the first time, the first sleep-over, climbing a tree, and so on). Then guide children back to the story with questions that encourage higher-level thinking.

* What are some ways the author makes this story seem real?

* What kind of person is Mirette? (Use a character web to record responses.)

* How do you think Mirette felt when she made it across the wire in the courtyard?

Word Watch:
Compound Cards

windmill   **daylight**
spotlight   **skylight**

Write these words on a chart and ask students if they notice anything special about them. (Each word is actually two words together.) Ask: "Do you know any other words like this?" Add new words to the chart. Let students play with compound words by making flap cards.

* Divide a piece of paper (about 8-by-3 inches) into three equal parts.

* Write a compound word in the center section. Draw a picture to go with it.

* Write the first part of the compound word in the first section, the second part in the third section. Illustrate each.

* Fold the first and last sections in to cover up the center section. Show how to unfold the flaps to uncover each part of the word.

* How do you think Mirette felt when she went out on the real high wire?

* Were you expecting the story to end the way it did? What was surprising to you?

Writer's Corner: I Can Do It!

Mirette's success in walking the high wire came with lots of practice. Invite children to tell their own stories of determination, writing about times they've worked hard to accomplish something. Begin by asking them to brainstorm a list of accomplishments that required practice (such as tying shoes, riding a bike, reading, whistling).

Let children team up with partners and talk about their accomplishments. (Have them each choose one.) Provide questions to guide their discussions. For example:

* What did you want to be able to do?

* How old were you? Did you know anyone who could do this?

* How did you practice? How often?

* Do you remember how you felt when you could finally do it?

Have children design posters (like the poster of Mirette and the Great Bellini in the story) to tell about their accomplishments. Display posters along with *Mirette on the High Wire*.

STORY EXTENSIONS

Science/Movement: A Balancing Act

Share the quote on page 92 then ask: "What do you think helped Mirette keep her balance?" Invite students to investigate their ideas by making a tightrope in the classroom. Place a length of masking tape on the floor or tape down several yardsticks end to end. Let children walk toe to heel from one end to the other, balancing objects on their heads, hopping, skipping, and so on. Explore the concept of balance further by trying these tightrope tests.

- ❈ Walk toe to heel with your arms out to your side.
- ❈ Walk toe to heel with a book in one hand, held out to the side, while your other arm is at your side.
- ❈ Walk toe to heel holding a book in both hands above your head.
- ❈ Walk toe to heel holding a book in both hands below your waist, close to your body.

Which was easiest? (The last way lowers your body's center of gravity and makes it easier to stay balanced.)

Art/Social Studies: Painting Masterpieces

[TIP] *Mix soap powder with tempera paint to form a thick mixture. Paper plates make fun palettes.*

Explore the expressive art of the post-impressionist period. Young children may enjoy looking at paintings by van Gogh, one of the artists from this time. Read *Van Gogh* by Ernest Raboff (HarperCollins, 1988) to learn more about the artist's life and see some of his paintings. Check with a museum for postcards, posters, and other material. Let children use the artist's work as inspiration for their own masterpieces. Try the recipe (left) to make paint that's as thick and colorful as the paint van Gogh preferred.

Social Studies: Who Are Our Heroes?

Mirette was inspired by the great Bellini to realize her dream of becoming a tightrope walker. Take a look at people students admire most. Help children distinguish between being famous and being a hero. Also stress that heroes may be people in our own lives, such as family members and friends.

Introduce children to heroes in history with a mini research project. Help children tailor their research by asking them to list interests and goals. For example, sports-minded children might like to learn about legends Lou Gehrig and Wilma Rudolph. Help children focus their research by answering these questions.

* Why is this person a hero to you?

* What five questions would you like to ask your hero?

* What challenges did your hero face?

Building on Books

Meet more book characters—fictional and real-life—who persevere in the face of great challenges. Three winning titles follow:

Lou Gehrig: The Luckiest Man by David Adler (Harcourt Brace, 1997). The author provides the kind of details that let readers get to know the person Lou Gehrig was—a man who never missed a day of school as a child, who never missed a game playing first base for the Yankees, a man who considered himself "the luckiest man on the face of the earth," even as he suffered from a degenerative disease.

Tillie and the Wall by Leo Leonni (Knopf, 1989). A young mouse is curious about what's on the other side of a wall and digs a tunnel to find out.

Wilma Unlimited: How Wilma Rudolph Became the World's Fastest Woman by Kathleen Krull (Harcourt Brace, 1996). After a serious childhood illness, doctors tell Wilma Rudolph she'll never walk again. Wilma refuses to believe it, and after years of hard work, goes on to become the first American woman to win three gold medals at a single Olympics.

Grandfather's Journey

WRITTEN AND ILLUSTRATED BY ALLEN SAY
(HOUGHTON MIFFLIN, 1993)

This is the story of a cross-cultural family. It begins with the author's memories of his grandfather, who left Japan for California, and eventually returned to Japan with his family. Though the grandfather was happy to be home in Japan, he missed the mountains and rivers he left behind. When his grandfather dies, the author, who grew up in Japan, decides to see the mountains and rivers his grandfather missed so much. He stays in California, but like his grandfather, never forgets his homeland.

The funny thing is, the moment I
am in one country,
I am homesick for the other.
I think I know my grandfather now.
I miss him very much.

—FROM *GRANDFATHER'S JOURNEY*

An Inside Look

Allen Say, who grew up in Japan and later moved to the United States, always dreamed of becoming an artist. As a boy, he worked four hours a day apprenticing with Noro Shinpei, a famous cartoonist. "What I really learned from this man was how an artist thought and how he lived his life, which was more important than learning how to draw." (From *Meet the Authors and Illustrators: Volume Two*)

An Art Lesson: Rock Garden Designs

Explore rock gardens—a part of Japanese culture that is woven into the illustrations in *Grandfather's Journey*. In Japan, rock gardens symbolize the beauty of the natural world—the earth, mountains, water, and so on. Let children look for rock gardens in the illustrations. Then have them work together to design a miniature rock garden for the classroom or school lobby.

Materials

☀ rocks

☀ tray-size sheets of cardboard

☀ plastic bowls, water, sand, small plants, paint (optional)

1 Take a walk with children to gather small rocks.

2 Set up rocks and other materials in a corner of the classroom. Let children visit a few at a time to design their rock gardens. For optional design elements, they can use small plastic bowls to create ponds, paint rocks blue to symbolize waterfalls, mold sand, and arrange plants.

3 Display rock gardens in the classroom, a corner of the library, or the lobby. Let them inspire students' appreciation of nature and their visual eye for art in the world around them.

Building on Books

Allen Say shares another glimpse into the life of a Japanese family with *Tree of Cranes* (Houghton Mifflin, 1993), the story of a mother who decorates a tiny tree with paper cranes to show her son how she celebrated Christmas as a child in America.

LANGUAGE ARTS LINKS

Book Talk

After reading the story, guide a discussion about the family's cross-cultural experiences.

☀ What do you think the grandfather liked most about California? What do you think he missed most about Japan?

☀ When the grandfather returned to Japan, how do you think he felt?

☀ What kinds of stories do you think the grandfather told the boy?

❋ When the boy grew up and moved to California, what do you think he missed about Japan?

❋ Have you ever moved from one place to another or taken a trip to a faraway place? (Note that *faraway* could be another country or the town down the road.) What did you like about the place you went to? What did you miss about the place you left behind?

Word Watch:
Family Words

grandfather

Add a family-word chart to your room's print resources, starting with the word *grandfather*. Reread the story, looking for and listing other family words (*daughter, grandparents*). Let children add to the chart with names for people in their own families, including parents, siblings, as well as more distant relatives. Encourage children to use the chart when they need family words in their own stories.

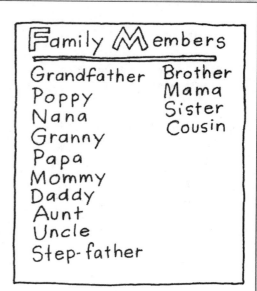

Family Members

Grandfather   Brother
Poppy   Mama
Nana   Sister
Granny   Cousin
Papa
Mommy
Daddy
Aunt
Uncle
Step-father

Traveling Words

[TIP] *Add a challenge by having children categorize the words before creating their dictionary pages—for example, grouping them by air, water, and land travel.*

The author's grandfather traveled from Japan to California by steamship. Ask: "How do you think the author made the same journey when he was old enough to travel?" Use chart paper to make a picture dictionary of transportation words. Let students suggest ways they have traveled as well as other modes of transportation. Write the words on the chart paper, leaving space for pictures. Let children draw or cut out pictures to go with the words. Add the dictionary to your classroom writing resources. Children can add to it as they discover new words.

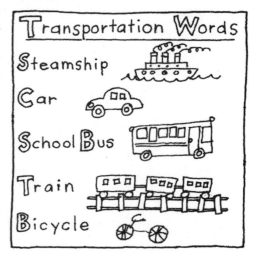

Transportation Words

Steamship
Car
School Bus
Train
Bicycle

Writer's Corner: My Journey

In *Grandfather's Journey*, the author tells of his grandfather's journey to America and what he loves most about his new home. Use the beginning of the story as a model for students' stories about their own journeys (such as a trip to the grocery store; a visit to a different city, state, or country; or a move). To guide their writing, use questions such as these that parallel the book:

* Where did you go?

* How did you travel?

* What did you bring with you?

* What were some of the first things you saw?

* What did you like best about the place you traveled to?

* What did you miss about home?

Possible formats for writing include postcards, journals, newspaper/magazine articles, and letters. (To extend this activity, see Family Travels, page 102.)

> **Dylan's Journey**
>
> I like to visit my cousin David's house. We have to drive a long way to get there. When we're there, I like to play in the treehouse. We climb up a ladder to get there. We fix things up there. I hand David wood and he hammers. I don't like to leave David's house. But when I'm there I miss my friends and my cat Pete.

STORY EXTENSIONS

Dramatic Play: Cultural Connections

Use the pictures in the story to inspire dramatic-play experiences. Stock your dramatic-play area with items that represent aspects of traditional Japanese culture.

* **kimonos:** Cut off the collars, cuffs, and buttons from large shirts.

* **obi:** Cut colorful fabric into long sashes for kimonos; wrap around the waist.

* **geta:** Traditional footwear—make by tracing children's feet on cardboard and stapling fabric strips or ribbon to create a thonglike sandal.

* **tatami:** Traditional straw mats—cut cardboard boxes into mat-size pieces and let children draw lines to represent woven material.

* **ikebana:** Supply artificial flowers, branches, vases, and

florist's clay and allow children to experiment with the traditional Japanese art of flower arranging.

❋ **fans:** Demonstrate how to bend paper back and forth to make an accordion-fold fan; staple at the bottom and add ribbon at the bottom to make a handle.

Let students sample Japanese food as they play one day. Rice, soba noodles, and bamboo shoots (available in the specialty food section of many grocery stores) are just a few of the foods you might serve.

Math: Paper Folding Fun

Material

❋ paper cut into 6-inch squares

[T I P] *If you use origami paper, have children start with the paper colored-side up. If you use white paper, you might invite children to color it before you begin. As students complete each fold, have them crease the edges.*

The art of origami utilizes geometry, fractions, and measurement in every design. Let children look at the origami boat pictured on the back cover of *Grandfather's Journey*. Then guide them in making their own simple boats.

Give each child a square of paper. Guide children in completing the following steps.

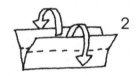

❋ Fold the paper in half, bottom edge to top edge. (1)

❋ Fold one of the top halves down so that the top and bottom edges meet. (2, 3)

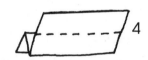

❋ Turn the paper over and again bring the top half down so that the top and bottom edges meet. Crease the edge then unfold. (3,4)

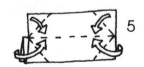

❋ Fold each corner (top and bottom) in. Fold the bottom layers together. (5)

❋ Fold the top edge down to meet the bottom edge. (6) Pull open the top edges and press down on the inside to shape the bottom of the boat. (7)

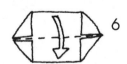

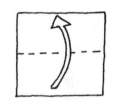

Social Studies/Language Arts: Family Travels

Build on the stories the grandfather told the boy about California by inviting children to ask grandparents (or other family members) about their journeys. Let children use the take-home journal page (see page 103) to gather information. Have them use their notes to write stories about the journeys. As children share their stories, use a map to locate destinations.

Art: Memory Time Lines

One of the illustrations in *Grandfather's Journey* pictures a favorite memory of the author's—weekends at his grandfather's. In *Meet the Authors and Illustrators: Volume Two*, Allen Say says, "All good artists have an excellent memory. You have to remember. You cannot imagine without memory." To inspire their artistic efforts, help students build a bank of memories by making memory time lines.

Materials

* pencils, crayons, markers
* craft paper or large sheets of white paper

[TIP] *You may want to assign step 1 as a take-home activity, asking parents to work with their children in recording these memories.*

1 Ask students to list memories. These might include trips, visits with favorite people, "firsts" (such as losing a first tooth or riding a two-wheeler), arrival of pets or siblings, moves, and so on.

2 Help children number their memories in chronological order by asking which happened first, next, and so on.

3 Share a sample map you've made (you can enlarge the one shown here). Give children each a large sheet of craft paper and ask them to make their own maps, filling in dates of events, labeling them, and drawing pictures to illustrate.

4 Talk about ways students can use their maps—for example, to get ideas for stories. Encourage children to add on to their maps to record new memories.

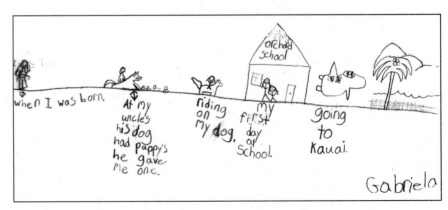

JOURNAL PAGE

Family Travels

Dear Parents,

We're reading *Grandfather's Journey* in class, a story about a grandfather who travels from Japan to America and the love he has for both places. Please help _____ find out about a journey someone in your family took. You can use the questions here to guide your child's investigation. Please have your child return the assignment by _____. Thank you.

Sincerely,

1. Who is the person you are writing about?

   _____

2. What journey did this person take?

   _____

3. How did he/she travel?_____

4. What did he/she bring on the trip? _____

5. What did this person like best about the place he/she went to?

   _____

6. What did this person miss most about home?

   _____

   _____

Smoky Night

WRITTEN BY EVE BUNTING
ILLUSTRATED BY DAVID DIAZ
(HARCOURT BRACE, 1994)

*Mama explains about
rioting. "It can happen
when people get angry.
They want to smash and
destroy. They don't care
anymore what's right and
what's wrong."*

—FROM *SMOKY NIGHT*

After the Los Angeles riots in 1992, Eve Bunting, author of more than 100 books for children, wondered about the children who live through such violent experiences. *Smoky Night* tells the story from a child's point of view—from windows breaking and people looting stores to cats and their owners being reunited after a fire. A book children can understand on many levels, *Smoky Night* shows how people who can't get along are brought together.

An Inside Look

David Diaz illustrated this evocative story by combining acrylic paintings on textured collage backgrounds. In his Caldecott acceptance speech, David Diaz explains the colors he selected for the characters. "One decision I made was to use the same color palette for all the characters in the story. I did this to avoid any indication of ethnic background, and to let their personalities speak for themselves."

An Art Lesson

Created from bits of cloth and paper, bubble wrap, matches, cardboard, small pieces of the illustrator's pottery, wood, and even cereal, the photographic collages in *Smoky Night* will capture your students' interest. Let them take a close look at each page. What other materials can they spot? Talk about possible reasons the illustrator might have had for choosing these materials. (For example, on the page that tells about a market being looted, cereal is spilled across the page.)

Let children experiment with collage to illustrate their own stories. Prepare by brainstorming materials children might use to illustrate familiar folktales—for example, red cloth, twigs, and flower petals for "Little Red Riding Hood," and straw, twigs, and small stones for "The Three Little Pigs." Talk about how the materials can help tell each story. Let children choose stories to illustrate. Then share basic collage procedures.

Materials

- ✳ large pieces of fabric and heavy paper (for collage backing)
- ✳ assorted collage materials
- ✳ white glue (it dries clear)
- ✳ paints and paintbrushes
- ✳ scissors

1 Let children select backings for their collages. If they choose to work on fabric, they might try fringing the edges to add texture.

2 Suggest that children experiment with placement before they begin to glue down materials.

3 Like David Diaz, children can paint pictures to use in their collages. Remind them to incorporate the paintings as they plan the placement of their materials.

LANGUAGE ARTS LINKS

Book Talk

The image of frightened cats "holding paws" is one that many children are drawn to. After you read the story again (your students will beg you to), let them share other memorable images. Then discuss the story, using something most children will be able to relate to—the cats—as a starting point. From there, you can guide the discussion to include more complicated issues, including what can happen when people get very angry and "...don't care anymore what's right and what's wrong." Questions to stimulate a discussion of these issues follow.

- ✳ What are some ways people in the story showed their anger? (They smashed windows, broke into stores and stole things, and so on.)

※ Why do you think some people in the story are crying? (They may be afraid; their stores may have been looted; they may be frightened by the fire.)

※ What do you think the cats' owners learned from their pets? (These cats, who had always fought with one another, stick together in the fire. When one owner expresses surprise, the child says, "They probably didn't know each other before…now they do." The owners decide maybe they need to get to know one another, too.)

Word Watch:
The Language of Feelings

angry

Can your students communicate feelings with words that are more specific than *happy, sad*, and *mad*? After reading the story, reread the quote on page 104. Ask children if they can find a feeling word in the quote. (*angry*) Explore other words for feelings by making a chart to record events, characters' feelings, and students' feelings. Together, list events in the story. One event at a time, ask students to suggest words for characters' feelings and their own. The chart here shows one way to begin.

Events	Characters' Feelings	Our Feelings
People are rioting.	Angry	Scared Nervous
There's a fire.	Scared Worried	
People go to a shelter.		

Writer's Corner: Story Sources

David Diaz and Eve Bunting make an award-winning team. (See Building on Books, page 107.) Let students team up to write and illustrate their own books together. For story ideas, they might try one of Eve Bunting's sources: the newspaper.

※ Cut out several different kinds of stories in advance and mount them on tagboard for easy handling. (Look for news stories, human interest stories, sports stories, letters to the editor, and so on.)

※ Share the stories with students, then use *who, what, why, where, when*, and *how* questions to guide discussions about the content.

※ Invite students to team up to retell the stories in picture-book format. Help children divide up tasks—for example, deciding who will write, draw, edit, and so on.

Building on Books

Many children will be drawn to the art in other books illustrated by David Diaz. Like *Smoky Night*, the following titles are illustrated with paintings on richly textured backgrounds. Just put the books within students' reach—and give them plenty of time to explore.

December, also by Eve Bunting (Harcourt Brace, 1997). A homeless mother and her son share their cardboard house one night with an old woman who has even less.

Wilma Unlimited: How Wilma Rudolph Became the World's Fastest Woman, by Kathleen Krull (Harcourt Brace, 1996). See page 96.

Both *December* and *Wilma Unlimited* provide wonderful opportunities for integrating character education in the classroom. Start a character web by writing one of the character's names in the center. Let children add words to tell what kind of person the character is. Follow up by letting children make character webs for people they know. What words describe their good qualities?

STORY EXTENSIONS

Dramatic Play: Anger Easers

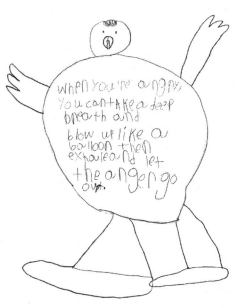

What are some ways children express anger? Reread the passage quoted on page 104 about anger. Then explore anger management with this simple activity. Invite children to share things that make them feel angry. Then brainstorm positive ways to handle that anger. William Kreidler, who leads teacher workshops in conflict resolution, suggests these anger easers in "The Caring Classroom" (*Instructor* Magazine, April 1996):

☀ Be a Balloon: Ask students to pretend they're balloons, and slowly fill themselves with air. Then ask them to slowly let it all out. Try it a few times. How does it feel?

☀ Down the Drain: From the tops of their heads to the tips of their toes, ask students to tense up every muscle in their bodies. Now have them relax each and every muscle. Feel those angry feelings drain down and out!

Follow up by having children work in teams to make posters about managing anger. Display them around school to help everyone learn more about managing this powerful feeling.

Social Studies: We're All Connected

Use the following game to help children understand the ways they are alike, despite any differences they may have.

- ☀ Start by making a statement like "Last weekend we went to see our friends in Boston."

- ☀ Invite a child to make a connection using something from your statement to build on his or her own—for example: "Once I went to Boston to see the aquarium."

- ☀ Let other children take turns building on each successive sentence—for example: "I have an aquarium with five fish and a turtle." "I went fishing on vacation with my uncle," and so on. When children get stuck, offer prompts.

- ☀ Play until children run out of connections—or until each child has made at least one.

Adapted from "The Caring Classroom" by William Kreidler, *Instructor* magazine, October 1995, by permission of *Instructor*.

Movement: Cooperation Lineup

The concept of cooperation is woven throughout *Smoky Night*. In the aftermath of the riots, two men work together to make sandwiches, a girl passes out hot chocolate, a firefighter returns missing cats to their owners. Together, they learn to get along and help each other out. To explore cooperation in the classroom, try this lineup game.

First, number a set of index cards from one to however many students you have. Put the cards in a bag. When it's time to line up for lunch, the gym, or some other activity, have children each draw a card from the bag and ask them to arrange themselves in order from lowest to highest number. (Build time into your schedule for this to happen.) Vary the lineup activity other days, asking children to line up according to birthdays, alphabetical order of first names, or some other criteria that requires them to cooperate.

Officer Buckle and Gloria

WRITTEN AND ILLUSTRATED BY PEGGY RATHMAN
(PUTNAM, 1995)

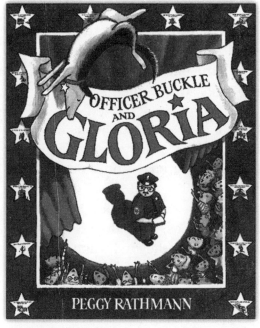

Safety Tip #101

*"ALWAYS STICK WITH
YOUR BUDDY!"*

— FROM *OFFICER BUCKLE
AND GLORIA*

With his police dog Gloria by his side, Officer Buckle goes from sharing safety tips with snoring students to being the most sought-after school visitor. Why? Unbeknownst to him, Gloria was stealing the show, performing antic after silly antic as Officer Buckle reads his tips. Just how much of an impact do the characters have on children? One teacher, standing on a swivel chair, was promptly told by students, "Mrs. Rea, you are doing exactly what Officer Buckle said not to do!"

An Inside Look

Winsome illustrations with plenty of detail (like the traffic signs on Officer Buckle's pajamas) support the text in a way that keeps children coming back to see what else they can discover. It's easy to see where the book's playful quality comes from. In her Caldecott acceptance speech, Rathman describes a writing class in which the teacher suggested letting embarrassing secrets inspire stories. "Weeks went by, and the other students began submitting stories. I developed the overwhelming urge to swipe their ideas. Eventually it occurred to me that this compulsion could be the embarrassing secret I'd been waiting for…" *Ruby the Copycat* (Scholastic, 1991) followed. Since then, she says, all of her books have been based on embarrassing secrets.

An Art Lesson

Use *Officer Buckle and Gloria* to introduce students to the way artists use light and shadow to add depth to illustrations.

Materials

* fine-point markers or pens
* paper
* paints and paintbrushes
* markers

1 Begin by noticing shadows in the classroom. Ask: "What do you notice about shadows?" For example, are they longer or shorter than the objects? Guide students to understand that a shadow occurs when an object blocks light. The closer an object is to the light source, the larger it will be.

2 Reread the book, asking students to notice shadows on the pages—formed by Officer Buckle and Gloria on the stage, seats in an auditorium, children at the ice cream stand, and so on. Can they find long shadows? Short shadows? Shadows in front of someone? Behind? Underneath?

3 Ask children to observe and draw shadows around them. Go a step further and invite children to draw their own scenes complete with shadows. Children who want to stick with the story can add onto the ending to show Officer Buckle and Gloria giving safety tips at their school.

Building on Books

Peggy Rathman's first book, *Ruby the Copycat* (Scholastic, 1991), is based on an urge she had to swipe classmates' writing ideas. The author says all of her books are based on embarrassing secrets. (See An Inside Look, page 109.) Ask: "What embarrassing secret do you think *Officer Buckle and Gloria* is about?" Let students try this writing idea themselves, using their own embarrassing moments as the basis for stories they write and illustrate.

LANGUAGE LINKS

Book Talk

Explore character and conflict with these questions.

* What kind of a person is Officer Buckle? How do you know?

* How do you think Officer Buckle feels about Gloria? What are some clues?

* What causes the problem in the story? (Officer Buckle discovers that Gloria has been stealing the show. His feelings are hurt.)

* How do Officer Buckle and Gloria work out their problem?

Writer's Corner: Tack Up a Tip!

Students will be eager to add to Officer Buckle's safety tips. Fill a basket with plenty of large paper stars (or provide a template and let children cut out their own), clear a bulletin board, and let students go to work writing and tacking up tips with push-pins. For the full effect, add a desk like Officer Buckle's for students to work at, a police cap (available at party stores), a candy jar (maybe filled with something more tasty than dog biscuits), and a play phone. Take your safety tips on tour, too, letting students share them with other classes.

Word Watch: Introducing Onomatopoeia

splat
splatter
sploosh

With these words, the author describes Napville School's biggest accident ever, one that starts with "a puddle of banana pudding...SPLAT! SPLATTER! SPLOOSH!" Use these words to introduce onomatopoeia—words that sound like their meaning. (Like *sploosh*, sometimes you need to make these words up!) After directing students' attention to the pudding scene in *Officer Buckle and Gloria*, give children an opportunity to practice spotting words that sound like their meaning. Read a list of words, including some that sound like their meaning (such as *drip, plop, pop, gurgle, ding-dong, boing, whoosh*). Ask children to tell you which ones sound like their meaning and which don't. Revisit onomatopoeia with *The Snowy Day*. (See page 43.)

STORY EXTENSIONS

Social Studies/Language Arts: Who Are Our Helpers?

Encourage children to learn more about the helpers in their own lives with this activity. With a disposable or inexpensive camera, children can take turns photographing school helpers, asking each to give a safety tip related to his or her work. (Record the helpers' names in order, along with their safety tips.) Have children work together to create a display with the photos, some cutting out star-shaped backgrounds to frame them, others writing out the safety tips like captions.

Movement: Pantomime Time

Copy children's safety tips on cards. (Add pictures too.) Let children take turns pretending to be Gloria, pantomiming tips for the audience. Who can guess the tip?

Social Skills: Puppets Solve Problems

Officer Buckle's buddy is Gloria. And even though they're friends, they had a problem to work out. Talk about what happened (Gloria was getting all the attention and Officer Buckle's feelings were hurt). Ask: "How did they handle it?" Then let children practice solving their own interpersonal problems.

1 Print friendship problems on cards. For example: Two friends are playing a game, and each one wants to go first.

2 Have children make simple stick puppets, taping pictures they draw or cut out to craft sticks or straws.

3 Let children take turns using the puppets to dramatize problems. Encourage them to experiment with different ways to solve the problems. Which ones do they think work best? Why?